DEAR,

May the Almighty bless you and your family
with his blessing.

Prophet Stories for Kids
Published by Hidayah Publishers

Copyright © 2022 Hidayah Publishers

PROPHET STORIES

Prophet Adam (A.S)

Prophet Nuh (A.S)

Prophet Ismael (A.S)

Prophet Yusuf (A.S)

Prophet Yunus (A.S)

Prophet Musa (A.S)

Prophet Suleman (A.S)

Prophet Isa (A.S)

Prophet Muhammad (P.B.U.H)

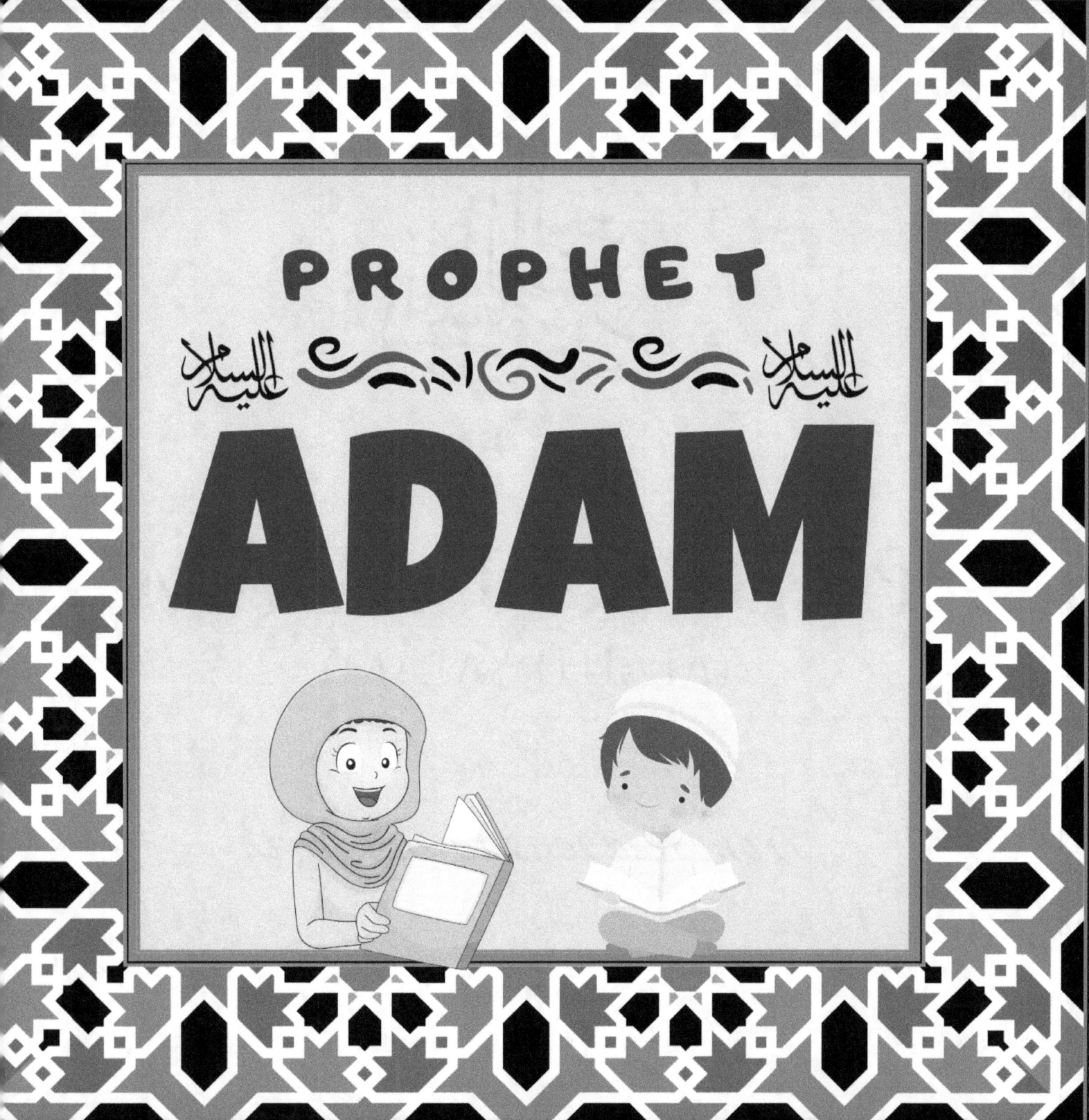

PROPHET ADAM

(ALAIHI SALAM)

From Heavens to the Earth

A long long time ago, Allah^Subhanahu wa Ta'ala created this Universe. This Universe was made with numerous heavenly bodies and seven skies. Among these, Allah created many species and beings. At that time, the Earth was dominated by the Jinns, and the skies were filled by obedient Angels. But regardless of these countless creatures, Allah decided to make a special living being. A being who will surpass all ranks in knowledge than the other creatures.

So, he asked his angels to collect clay from the Earth. The obedient Angels collected clay and Allah made a man-like figure with it and named him Adam^alayhis-salam.

But the figure didn't move for forty long years. It just stood still there. When Iblees, who was like a teacher of the Angels at that time, saw this figure, he was confused and scared.

After forty years, Allah^Subhanahu wa Ta'ala breathed his spirit into Adam^alayhis-salam. When the spirit reached the head of the figure. It's sneezed. When the spirit reached his eyes, he saw all the amazing food lying around. Then the spirit reached his stomach and Adam^alayhis-salam felt hungry. The Prophet had seen the fruits lying around, so before the spirit could even reach his legs, he jumped towards the fruit. Adam^alayhis-salam came down as he couldn't move his legs. Allah gave Adam^alayhis-salam vast knowledge of the things. Allah taught Adam^alayhis-salam the names of every animal in Paradise. The Lion, the sheep, the camel, Elephant, dog, peacock and many many more.

Then Allah^{Subhanahu wa Ta'ala} asked all the Angels including Iblees to prostrate before Adam^{alaihi Salam} as a sign of respect. One by one, all the Angels prostrated before the Prophet except Iblees.

Iblees said that he was better and superior to the Prophet and he was made from fire. He didn't understand the will of Allah and refused to obey Allah's command.

Allah^{Subhanahu wa Ta'ala} got angry with this disobedience. So, he banished Iblees from paradise. From that day, Iblees was called as 'the Satan/Shaitaan ' and he was thrown into the hell. He was now an outcast. Shaitaan was now furious with the humans as he was banished from the paradise because of them. He vowed to take revenge by misleading the humans in the way of Allah.

Allah^{Subhanahu wa Ta'ala} told the Prophet Adam^{alaihi Salam} that he was allowed to eat every fruit in the garden except one. Allah told the Prophet that he should not eat the fruit of the tree of knowledge, as it was forbidden. He spent most of his time playing with the animals in Paradise. After a few years, the prophet became lonely as there were no other humans in Paradise. Allah^{Subhanahu wa Ta'ala} saw this so he decided to give Adam^{alaihi Salam} a wife.

One night when the Prophet was sleeping, God created the first woman, Hawwa (Eve). When the Prophet woke up, he was happy to see the woman. His loneliness immediately went away.

Adam^{alaihi Salam} asked, "who are you?"

"Allah created me, so that you can find your peace and tranquility with me." she replied.

Allah^{Subhanahu wa Ta'ala} said to them, "Eat from this paradise, anything you desire." Both of them lived happily in Paradise for forty years. But Allah^{Subhanahu wa Ta'ala} warned them to not even go near to that 'Forbidden Tree'.

Many years had passed by. So Shaitaan knew that the Prophet must have forgotten the words of Allah. Shaitaan was still angry at the humans. He entered Jannah and tricked them to eat from that tree by falsely swearing by Allah. Shaitaan said that If you eat from that tree, you will become like Angels. You will become immortals. Think about it.

Adam^{alaihi Salam} never heard anyone lie in his life, so they both fell for it. The Prophet and his wife unknowingly plucked the fruit and started eating it. But even before they could finish eating the fruit, they knew they had committed a grave sin. They are now filled with pain, sadness, and shame. They realized they were naked. For they ran to cover themselves up in leaves. They were now really scared as they knew Allah would punish them for their disobedience.

Allah^{Subhanahu wa Ta'ala} said, "Didn't I warned you from eating from this tree? That the Shaitaan is your open enemy."

They said, "O our Lord! We have wronged ourselves. And if you don't have mercy on us, if you don't forgive us, then we will be of the losers."

They realized their mistake, but it was too late. And now they had to bear, what will happen to them. So, they got send down to the Earth. They came down to Earth in separate places. And so, they began the search for one and other. They became acquainted, they found each other on the mountain of Arafat. There they renewed their lives on Earth. They finally settle down near a river.

The prophet knew that life on Earth would be very difficult. He had to make a house for them to live. He had to work hard to feed his family. They now no longer had the pleasures they enjoyed in Paradise.

After a few years, Hawwa gave birth to twins, a boy and a girl. They named the boy 'Qabil'. Qabil was not very handsome whereas Qabil's twin sister was beautiful. Later, Hawwa gave birth to another twin. Again, a boy and a girl. This time, they name the boy 'Habil'. Habil was a little bit more handsome but his twin sister wasn't as attractive.

Both Habil and Qabil grew up. Qabil took to farming, working in the field and growing crops. When Habil grew up, he became a shepherd and took care of the sheep. When Habil and Qabil grew up to become adults, the Prophet Adam[alaihi Salam] decided to get them married. Since there were no other females on Earth, Prophet decided to get Qabil, married to Habil's twin sister and Habil to Qabil's twin sister.

Qabil was not happy as Habil's sister was not that beautiful. He wanted to marry his own sister. There was an argument, so the Prophet Adam[alaihi Salam] brought them together and settled the issue by offering a sacrifice to Allah[subhanahu ta'ala]. It was decided that the one whose sacrifice is accepted, will marry Qabil's sister.

Habil collected the finest and best sheep from his flock and offered it as a sacrifice to Allah^subhanahu ta'ala. But Qabil didn't want to offer the best fruit and vegetable as the sacrifice. Instead, He chose the bad vegetables and grains for sacrifice. Allah^Subhanahu wa Ta'ala accepted the sacrifice of Habil but rejected the one made by Qabil. The Prophet Adam^alaihi Salam was present when they made their sacrifices and it was decided that Habil would marry Qabil's sister. Qabil was not at all happy. He was so angry that he wanted to kill Habil.

One day Habil was late coming home and the Prophet ask Qabil to search for him. Qabil went searching to the fields for Habil. At last, He found Habil walking towards home. Qabil was still angry with Habil.

"Your offering was accepted but mine was not." said by Qabil.

Habil replied, " Allah^Subhanahu wa Ta'ala only accepts from those who fear Him."

Qabil was angry to hear this, and he picked up a stone to hit Habil. Habil saw this and even though he was bigger and stronger than Qabil but Habil piety to Allah^Subhanahu wa Ta'ala stopped him. He said, "Even if you stretch your hand to kill me, I will never stretch my hand to harm you because I fear Allah."

This comment further angered Qabil, and he struck him with the stone instantly killing him. When Qabil realized that Habil was dead, he was terrified and didn't know what to do. He didn't want his father to know what he has done. So, he started thinking about ways to hide his sin. Qabil wandered from place to place with the dead body of Habil, trying to hide it.

That was when he saw two crows fighting with each other. During the fight, one crow killed the other and the dead one fell down.

The victorious crow scratched and dug a hole in the ground. He buried the dead crow in the hole. Then he filled the hole with mud. This gave Qabil the idea, and like the crows, he dug a hole in the ground and buried his brother's body in it.

This was the first burial of a man. Qabil was ashamed of what he had done. He regretted, but he did not repent. He did not ask Allah[Subhanahu wa Ta'ala] for forgiveness. Shaitaan had won over him and he knew that he could no longer go back to his family.

The news came to their mother, Hawwa first. Then she started to cry. The Prophet Adam[alaihi Salam] knew what had happened, and he mourned at the loss of his son. He had lost both his sons; one was dead, and shaitaan misled the other. He warned his other children about shaitaan and ask them to always obey the commands of Allah[subhanahu ta'ala].

The Prophet Adam[alaihi Salam] had grown old and his children loved him very much. When Prophet Adam[alaihi Salam] realized that his death was near, he appointed Seth[alaihi Salam] as the successor to his family.

He said to his children: "O my children, indeed I feel an appetite for the fruits of Paradise."

So, they went away searching for what Adam[alaihi Salam] had requested. They met with the angels, who had with them his blanket and what he was to be embalmed with.

Angels said to them: "O Children of Adam, what are you searching for? What do you want? Where are you going?"

They said: "Our father is sick and has an appetite for the fruits of Paradise."

The angels said to them: "Go back, for your father is going to meet his end soon."

So, they returned with the angels. When Hawwa saw them, she recognized them. She tried to hide herself behind Adam^{alaihi Salam}.

"Leave me alone. I came before you; do not go between me and the angels of my Lord." He said.

Then, the Angel of Death stood beside him. He gathered his children on his death bed and reminded them saying,

"Allah^{Subhanahu wa Ta'ala} will send Messengers to you. He will not leave you alone. The prophets would have different names, traits and miracles, but they would be united in one thing, their message will all be one; the call to worship Allah alone; the one who made you. And to stay away from the Shaitaan. The biggest sin one can commit is to associate a partner with the creator."

After he reminded his children, the Angel of Death took his soul away. He passed away peacefully. He was happy to go because he knew he was going back to Allah^{subhanahu wa ta'ala}. As Prophet Muhammad^{sallallaho alaihi wasallam} said, "The gift of a true believer is death."

His sons embalmed and wrapped him, dug the grave and laid him in it. They prayed for him and put him in his grave, saying:

"O Children of Adam, this is your tradition at the time of death."

PROPHET NUH

(ALAIHI SALAM)

When Floods drowned All Humanity on Land

Allah^{subhanahu wa ta'ala} sent Prophet Nuh (Noah)^{alaihi salam} to Earth, thousand years after sending Prophet Adam ^{alaihi salam}. By then, the population on Earth had increased many folds and by this time the evil 'Shaitaan' had played his dirty tricks on mankind and made people start worshipping idols. It was during this time that Allah ^{subhanahu wa ta'ala} sent another Prophet to Earth.

Prophet Nuh ^{alaihi salam} guided the people back to the worship of one God, Allah ^{subhanahu wa ta'ala}, but it would not be an easy job for the Prophet. Nuh ^{alaihi salam} was an excellent speaker and a very patient man. He pointed out to his people the mysteries of life and the wonders of the universe. He pointed out how the night is regularly followed by the day and that the balance between these opposites were designed by Allah the Almighty for our good. The night gives coolness and rest while the day gives warmth and awakens activity. The sun encourages growth, keeping all plants and animals alive, while the moon and stars assist in the reckoning of time, direction and seasons. He pointed out that the ownership of the heavens and the earth belongs only to the Divine Creator.

Therefore, he explained to this people, there cannot have been more than one deity. He clarified to them how the devil had deceived them for so long and that the time had come for this deceit to stop. Nuh ^{alaihi salam} spoke to them of Allah's glorification of man, how HE had created him and provided him with sustenance and the blessings of a mind. He told them that idol worshipping was a suffocating injustice to the mind. He warned them not to worship anyone but Allah and described the terrible punishment Allah would mete out if they continued in their evil ways.

"Fear Allah and do what Allah says!" shouted the Prophet to everyone.

But the people didn't want to listen. They shook their heads and continued worshipping the idols. The Prophet was an excellent speaker, and he was very patient too.

"Don't you understand that it was Allah who created this entire world!" shouted the Prophet. "It was Allah who created the Sun, the moon, and the stars you see in the sky. He created the rivers, the mountains, the trees, and everything you see around. He did all this for you, and you alone. Then why are you not showing him any respect? Why are you worshiping these Idols?"

But the people turned their backs on him saying,

"Huh! Who are you to advise us? You're just another man. And we think that you're lying. Go away and leave us alone!"

But there were good Muslims on Earth too, but most of them were weak and poor. They listen to the words of the Prophet and realized that they were committing a sin by worshipping the idols.

Now, there were two different groups of people on Earth; one who worship Allah subhanahu wa ta'ala and the others who continued idol worshipping.

Nuh alaihi salam continued preaching to the people for many years. The idol-worshippers soon became exhausted by the preaching of the Prophet.

"You've been preaching lies for long enough." they said, "We will stone you if you do not stop."

But the Prophet ignored them and continued calling the people tirelessly towards to Allah. He preached to them during the day and the night. On many occasions, the idol worshippers stoned him while preaching to the crowd. They even beat him with the sticks.

"You are no different from us!" shouted the idol worshippers. "You are no Prophet. You are just another man. And why should we listen to you?"

"I'm telling you the truth." the Prophet said to them. "You are committing a sin by worshipping the idols."

"I fear for you! Allah is going to punish you one day!" the Prophet shouted to them.

But the people had no shame. They said, "He is a fool, don't listen to him."

All this pain did not let the Prophet Nuh alaihi salam to stop calling out to the people. He continued preaching to them for nine hundred and fifty years. The disbelievers kept making fun of the Prophet and by now, they had taken things too far. Nuh alaihi salam was disappointed, whereas the number of disbelievers kept growing and growing. One night, when the Prophet was offering his players, Allah subhanahu wa ta'ala spoke to him.

"Don't be sad, Nuh."

"You have done what you were asked to. I am going to punish all the people on Earth for their wrongdoings. Everyone on Earth will die except the believers and the animals." said Allah subhanahu wa ta'ala.

As the first step, God asked the Prophet to plant several trees. Nuh^{alaihi salam} didn't understand the reason behind this but he listened to Allah and started planting trees as he was told. He also asked the believers to listen to him and to do the same. They did this for more than a hundred years.

After many years, Allah^{subhanahu wa ta'ala} commanded the Prophet again. This time, he asked the Prophet to start building a ship. It has to be a gigantic ship that can accommodate a pair of every animal on the Earth.

The Prophet was confused as he didn't know how to build a ship because no one had ever made a ship before. Despite this, the Prophet started making the ship with the help of his disciples. First, they made plans for building the ship. Some say that it had a length of six hundred feet, and others say that it had a length of twenty-four hundred feet. Whatever it was, the ship would sure be a gigantic one.

"We will help you to build the ship." said his children and the believers, and they joined the Prophet. First, the prophet had to choose a place for building the ship. He chose the mountains far far away from the city. The Prophet collected the tools and set out to build the ship. They started cutting down the trees for wood. Yes! It was the same trees he had planted more than a hundred years back. Then they started building the ship as per the plan. The men worked very hard, day and night to build the ship.

When the disbeliever saw them building a ship on the top of a mountain, they started making fun of them. "Haha! you are such an old fool," they said. "Why would you possibly need a ship so huge?" the other said. "And how are you going to take it to the sea?"

"You would come to know very soon." replied the Prophet Nuh^{alaihi salam}. The people didn't know why the Prophet was building the ship. They thought that he had lost his mind.

The Prophet and his men kept working hard. After many months, the ship was finally ready. They thanked Allah^{subhanahu wa ta'ala} for helping them to finish the ship. The time for the flood was nearing day by day. One night, Allah told the Prophet that he will start flooding the Earth the day when the Prophet sees water coming out of the stove in his house.

This huge ship built by the Prophet had three different sections. It's for different types of animals. The topmost one was for Birds. The second part of the structure was for humans, and the third part was for the animals.

As the day of the flood got nearer, animals, and the birds started arriving one by one. They were arriving in pairs, one male and one female. There were elephants, giraffes, lions, rabbits, and different species of birds. Soon, the ship was filled with all the variety of animals and birds from the earth.

One day, like Allah^{subhanahu wa ta'ala} had told the Prophet Nuh^{alaihi salam}, water suddenly started coming out of the stove in his kitchen. This was the sign Nuh^{alaihi salam} was waiting for. He understood that the time of the flood had arrived. When he went out, he saw that it had started raining too. Wasting no time, he ran out and called all the believers who had helped him to build the ship. He asked all of them to board the ship at once.

The disbelievers didn't understand what was going on. So, they kept laughing at the Prophet and his disciples.

"Look at these fools!" they said. "What is he going to do with all those animals and people?"

The Prophet ignored them and asked his wives and sons to board the ship quickly. Everyone obeyed him except for one of his wives and her son, who are not his followers.

"I will save myself from the water." his son said. "Don't worry about me."

The water levels have gone up by now. So, the Prophet Nuh^alaihi salam run to board the ship. A terrible flood broke out and the water levels rose rapidly. The Earth's crust moved and the ocean floor started rising, which caused it to flood the drylands. The rain didn't stop for hours, either.

By then, people had realized that what the Prophet told them was certainly true. They ran towards the mountains to save themselves. The Prophet saw that his wife and son, climbing a mountain to escape from the water. So, he shouted to them,

"Come on! Board the ship! Save yourself!"

But they ignored him and climb to the top of the mountain. Then an enormous wave, bigger than the mountain they stood on, came and hit them. These enormous waves swept away and killed all the disbelievers. The water kept rising and rising, and after some time, the Earth was completely filled with water.

Then Prophet Nuh^alaihi salam said "Bismillah!"

When the Prophet uttered these words, the ship started moving. The rains had stopped by now, but the entire Earth was filled with water. The Prophet knew that he had to keep sailing for a long long time. The ship had eighty people in it and the Prophet had taken precautions to store enough food for the people and the animals. Allah^subhanahu wa ta'ala had it all planned. He made the ship suitable for the silent sheep as well as the violent lion. All the violent animals were down with some or the other sickness.

All of them were living together, but the Prophet faced a lot of trouble because of the rats. They were everywhere running up and down, nibbling here and there. They were really the troublemakers, so the Prophet prayed to God and it was then, Allah created the cats.

The cats hunted down the rats, and after some time, the rats started behaving as well. It was difficult to sustain with all the other species in the confined space of a ship but Allah^subhanahu wa ta'ala solved many problems that the Prophet Nuh^alaihi salam had to face during the journey.

They sailed for about one-hundred-fifty days but couldn't find land anywhere they could see. The Prophet along with the believers, waited and waited for many days. Nuh^alaihi salam then decided to send a big crow to see if he could find land anywhere but the crow didn't return at all. Then, the Prophet sent a dove in search of the land. The dove flew away and after a few days, returned with a branch of the olive tree in its beaks.

The Prophet and his disciples were thrilled, as they knew that they were close to the land. The ship sailed further for some time and finally reached on the top of the 'Mount Judi'.

Nuh^alaihi salam said 'Bismillah!' and the ship stopped moving. With the issue of the divine command, calm returned to earth, the water retreated, and the dry land shone once again in the rays of the sun. The flood had cleansed the earth of the disbelievers and polytheists.

After traveling for over one-hundred fifty days, their journey had finally come to an end. The Prophet and other believers came out of the ship. And the first thing he did, was to put his forehead to the ground in prostration. The Prophet released all the animals, birds, and insects first, into the land. The survivors kindled a fire and sat around it. Lighting a fire had been prohibited on the ship so as not to ignite the ship's wood and burn it up. None of them had eaten hot food during the entire period of the floor. Following the disembarkation there was a day of fasting in thanks to Allah^{subhanahu wa ta'ala}.

They went out and populated the Earth back again. That was a fresh beginning for the human race and the Earth began to populate again.

"Except for those who are patient and do righteous deeds; those will have forgiveness and great reward." [Hud 11:11]

PROPHET ISMAEL

(ALAIHI SALAM)

The Story of Sacrifice

TOWARDS THE DESERTED DESTINATION

After Allah[(S.W.T)] blessed Prophet Ibrahim[(A.S)] with a child, he was instructed after some time to move on towards a place with his wife and son. He woke up and told his wife Hajara[(R.A)] to get her son and prepare for a long journey. The child was still nursing and not yet weaned.

Prophet Ibrahim[(A.S)] walked through cultivated land, desert, and mountains until he reached the desert of the Arabian Peninsula, and came to an uncultivated valley having no fruit, no trees, no food, no water. The valley had no sign of life, and it was a very very hot place. After Ibrahim[(A.S)] had helped his wife and child to dismount, he left them with a small amount of food and water which was hardly enough for two days. He turned around and walked away. His wife hurried after him asking: "Where are you going Ibrahim, leaving us in this barren valley?"

Ibrahim[(A.S)] did not answer her but continued walking. She repeated what she had said, but he remained silent. Finally, she understood that he was not acting on his own initiative. She realized that Allah had commanded him to do this. She asked him:

"Did Allah command you to do so?" He replied: "Yes." Then his great wife said: "We are not going to be lost since Allah Who has commanded you is with us."

Hajara(R.A) went on suckling Ismael(A.S) and drinking from the water she had. When the water in the waterskin had been used up, she became thirsty and her child also became thirsty. She started looking at his son tossing in agony.

She said to herself: "No, I must make an effort to try and look for some food."

She left him, for she could not endure looking at him, and found that the mountain of 'As-Safa' was the nearest mountain to her on that land. She went up the mountain and started looking at the valley keenly so that she might see somebody, but nobody was there till the horizon.

Then she descended 'As-Safa' calling to Allah for help. When she reached the valley, she tucked up her robe and ran in the valley like a person in distress and trouble, till she crossed the valley and reached the mountain of 'Al-Marwa'. There she stood and started looking expecting to see somebody, but she could not see anybody. She prayed to Allah for sustenance and repeated that running between As-Safa And Al-Marwa seven times.

The Prophet Muhammad(S.A.W.W) said:

"This is the source of the tradition of the Sa'ye, (rituals of the Hajj, pilgrimage) the running of people between mountains (As-Safa and Al-Marwa)."

When she reached Al-Marwa for the last time, she heard a voice and asked herself to be quiet and listened attentively.

She heard the voice again and said: "O whoever you maybe! You have made me hear your voice; have you got something to help me?"

And behold! She saw an angel, digging the earth with his heel (or his wing) till water streamed from that place. After expressing thanks to Allah Almighty, she started to make something like a basin around it and started filling her waterskin. She was saying 'zam-zam', means 'stop-stop flowing water'.

The Prophet Muhammad(S.A.W.W) said:

"May Allah bestow mercy on Ismael's mother! Had she let the zam-zam flow without trying to control it, or had she not scooped from that water to fill her water skin, Zam-zam would have been a stream flowing on the surface of the earth."

Then she drank water and suckled her child. The angel said to her: "Don't be afraid of being neglected, for this is the House of Allah which will be built by this boy and his father, and Allah never neglects His people." The Ka'ba at that time was on a high place resembling a hillock, and when torrents came, they flowed to its right and left.

In that era, when caravans passed through those deserts, they used to look for birds as a sign of the presence of the water. So, the clan of 'Jurhum' was passing near that valley and they noticed some birds in the middle of nowhere. They were not expecting them, probably they had traveled before and knew that in this region there is no water body.

They decided to send one of their men to follow the birds to the water destination. He reached near the valley of Makkah and saw Bibi Hajara(R.A) with her child. He went back to his people and explained the situation. They were very amazed by the presence of gushing water in the valley.

They reached and asked Bibi Hajara(R.A), "Do you mind if we live here?"

She realized that these people have good character, and they are civilized and cultured.

She said to them, "You can live here, and benefit from this water as you like but it is our property, not yours. This water belongs to us."

They made the valley their place of living and were very happy by the generosity of Bibi Hajara(R.A). Prophet Ismael(A.S) brought up among them and they loved him so much. They were pure Arabs, so they taught him Arabic. In the meanwhile, his father, Prophet Ibrahim(A.S) used to visit them occasionally. He was quite happy seeing the people living in harmony in the valley.

THE TRIAL OF SACRIFICE

Once, when Prophet Ibrahim(A.S) was staying in Makkah, he had a dream.

He saw himself slaughtering his son Ismael.

Prophet Ibrahim(A.S) was in a very tough position, as it was a great test for the Prophet as a father.

"Slaughter your son." The divine command said.

The Prophet said in obedience, "O Allah! We heard and we obey, regardless of what you order."

He knew that Allah's order must be implemented. The following day, Prophet Ibrahim(A.S) related the dream to his son.

"O my son, I have been instructed in a dream by Allah(S.W.T) to sacrifice you. So, what do you think I should do?"

Prophet Ismael(A.S) replied, "O my father, do as Allah has commanded you. You will find me from amongst those who are patient."

This shows the obedience of the Prophets to Allah's will. A true heart who fears Allah and obey him.

Then, Prophet Ibrahim(A.S) took Ismael(A.S) away from his mother and looked for a place to slaughter his son. On the way, Iblees came and tried to turn away Ibrahim(A.S) from fulfilling Allah's order.

Iblees said: "O Ibrahim! Are you really going to slaughter your own son? You just saw a dream; maybe it was just a dream."

Prophet Ibrahim^(A.S) grabbed stones and threw at him. Iblees then tried to shake Ismael's^(A.S) decision, so he also stoned Iblees. This act became the part of Hajj where Muslims throw those three different throws, as a memory that when you attempt to do something for Allah, be firm and strong.

Both Father and the son found a big rock, suitable to lay Ismael^(A.S) on it and slaughter him.

Ismael^(A.S) knew the affection of his father towards him, so he said:

"O father! Make my face towards the ground, so in case if you look at my face while you are slaughtering, you might overwhelm with sympathy and stop sacrificing me. Sharpen your knife, so you could slaughter me quickly, fulfilling the order of Allah^(S.W.T)."

Now, when Ibrahim^(A.S) grabbed the knife, put it on Ismael^(A.S) neck, and started to slaughter him, the knife spin the other side. He tried again but the knife didn't cut the throat of Ismael^(A.S). because it was Allah's order to the knife not to cut.

Prophet Ibrahim^(A.S) tried one last time with full power and the knife started cutting the neck, but it was not the neck of Prophet Ismael^(A.S). Allah^(S.W.T) replace Ismael^(A.S) with a ram from paradise. Ibrahim^(A.S) looked and saw that it was a ram.

Allah called out to Ibrahim^(A.S):

"O Ibrahim! You are indeed truthful to us. We have tested you and you have passed the test. Indeed, this was a clear trial."

Both Father and the son passed the ultimate test.

THE FOUNDATION OF KA'BAH

The days went passed. Prophet Ibrahim(A.S) stayed away from them for a period as long as Allah wished and then one day another order came from Allah(S.W.T); to build a house as a symbol of the oneness of Allah Almighty.

So, Ibrahim(A.S) went to the valley of Makkah and he saw Ismael(A.S) sitting under a tree near Zam-Zam, sharpening his arrows. When Ismael(A.S) saw his father, he rose to welcome him, and they greeted each other as a father does with his son or a son does with his father.

Ibrahim(A.S) said: "O Ismael! Allah has given me an order."

Ismael(A.S) replied, "Do what your Lord has ordered you to do."

"Will you help me?"

Ismael(A.S) said, "Yes, I will help you."

Ibrahim(A.S) said: "Allah has ordered me to build a house here," pointing to a hillock higher than the land surrounding it.

Then they raised the foundations of the House (the Ka'bah). Prophet Ismael(A.S) brought the stones while Prophet Ibrahim(A.S) built the walls. When the walls became high, Ismael(A.S) brought a stone and put it for Ibrahim(A.S), who stood over it and carried on building. When it became further high, Allah(S.W.T) caused the rock on which Ibrahim(A.S) standing, to raise when placing the rock and descend when Ibrahim(A.S) needed to pick another rock.

إسْمَاعِيل
(ʾIsmāʿīl)

While Ismael^(A.S) was handing him the stones, both of them were saying:

"Our Lord! Accept this service from us, verily, you are the All-Hearer, the All-Knower." (Ch 2:127-Quran)

And when the house was built, there was a corner left to fix a rock. Ibrahim^(A.S) thought to himself,

"I had to put a proper rock in this corner that fits and completes the wall."

Ismael^(A.S) went looking for the rock but he couldn't find it. When he came back, he saw a beautiful rock there.

Ibrahim^(A.S) said, "Allah sent me a rock from Jannah."

This is the rock that we call today "Al-Hajar Al-Aswad". It was white at that time but became black from the sins of people.

Through time, civilization and settlements started to take place in the valley of Makkah. Prophet Ismael^(A.S) mingled with the Yemeni tribe 'Jurhum' and became fluent in the Arabic language, delivering the message of Allah^(S.W.T) to the people. From the offspring of Prophet Ismael^(A.S), tribe 'Quraish' comes, and from Quraish, 'Hashim' comes. Abdul Mutallib^(R.A) was a 'Hashmi', who is the grandfather of Prophet Muhammad^(S.A.W.W).

Allah^(S.W.T) describes the beautiful characteristics of Prophet Ismael^(A.S) in the Qur'an,

"And mention in the Book, Ismael. Indeed, he was true to his promise, and he was a messenger and a prophet. And he used to enjoin on his people prayer and zakah, and was pleasing to his Lord."

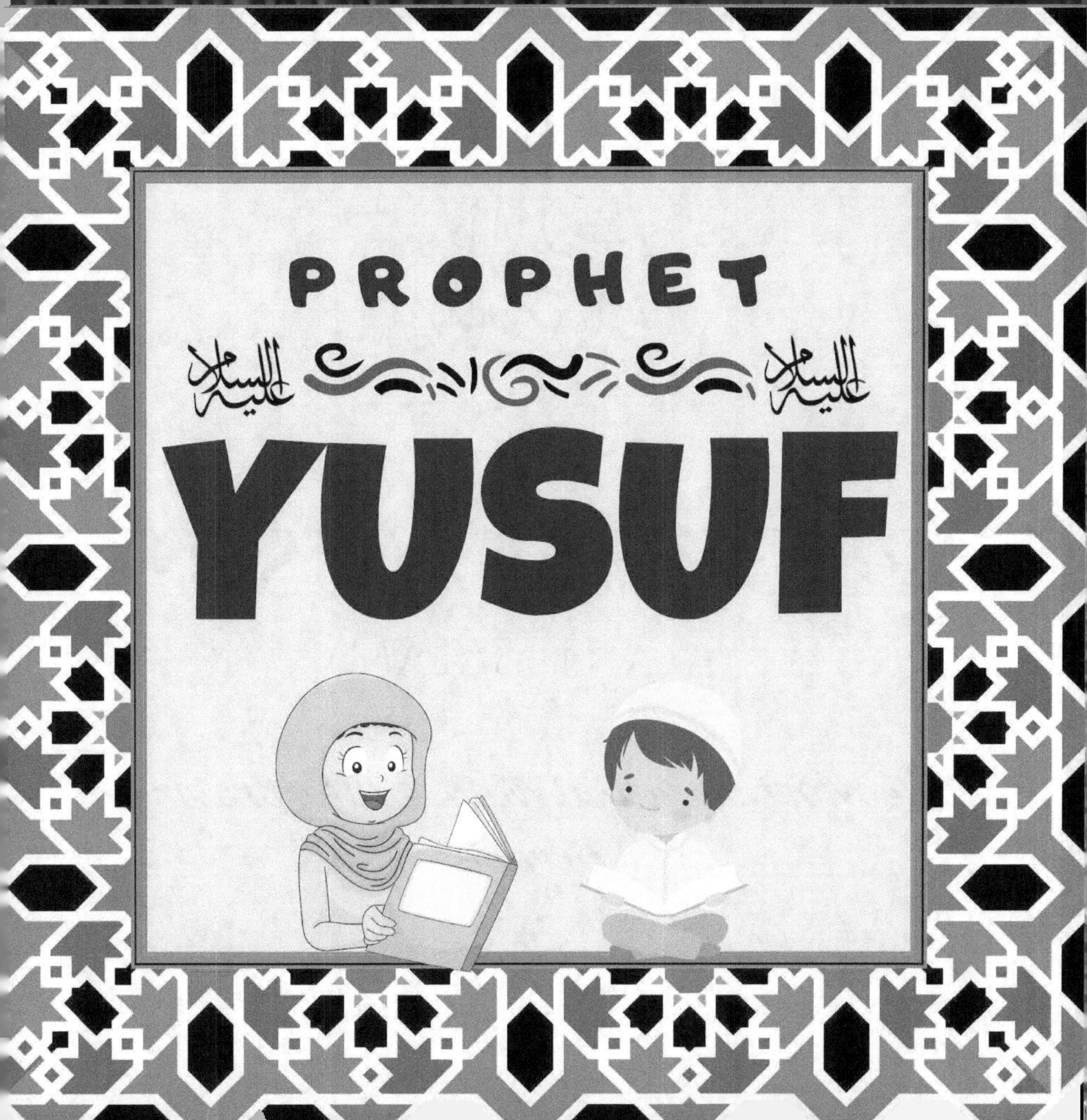

PROPHET

عليه السلام ~~~~~~ عليه السلام

YUSUF

PROPHET YUSUF

(ALAIHI SALAM)

The Most Beautiful Man & Interpreter of Dreams

This is the most detailed and fascinating story in the Quran, involving both human weaknesses, such as jealousy, hatred, pride, passion, deception, intrigue, cruelty, and terror, as well as noble qualities, such as patience, loyalty, bravery, nobility, and compassion.

It is related that among the reasons for its revelation is that the Jews asked the Prophet Muhammad^{sallallaho alaihi wasallam} to tell them about Prophet Joseph/Yusuf^{alaihi salam}, who was one of their old Prophets. His story had been distorted in parts and flawed in others with interpolation and exclusions. Therefore, it was revealed in the Qur'an-the last and authentic book of Allah^{subhanahu wa ta'ala}- complete in its minute and careful details.

Yusuf^{alaihi salam} lived all his life confronting schemes made by the people closest to him. The story of Prophet Yusuf^{alaihi salam} inspires you with a feeling for the depth of Allah's power, supremacy, and the execution of His rulings despite the challenge of human intervention.

"And Allah has full power and control over his affairs, but most of men know not." (Ch 12:21)

THE DREAM

Prophet Yusuf[alaihi salam] was the son of Prophet Yaqoob[alaihi salam] and Rahel. He had a younger brother named Binyamin. Yaqoob[alaihi salam] had twelve sons in total. He loved Yusuf[alaihi salam] and Binyamin more than his other children. This made the other brothers very angry towards them.

The story begins with a dream and ends with its interpretation. As the sun appeared over the horizon, bathing the earth in its morning glory, Yusuf[alaihi salam] awoke from his sleep, delighted by a pleasant dream he had.

Filled with excitement, he ran to his father and related it.

"I saw eleven stars in the sky, and the sun, and the moon. They were all bowing down before me." He told his father.

The young Prophet was quite amazed by this dream. He wondered why stars bowed before him. He didn't understand the meaning. Yaqoob[alaihi salam] was a Prophet, and he understood the meaning of the dream. And he was very happy. His face lit up. He foresaw that Yusuf[alaihi salam] would be one through whom the prophecy of his grandfather, Prophet Ibrahim[alaihi salam] would be fulfilled, in that his offspring would keep the light of Ibrahim's house alive and spread Allah's message to mankind.

"Allah[subhanahu wa ta'ala] has blessed you, Yusuf." The old Prophet told his son. "This dream means that you will be given knowledge and prophecy."

Yaqoob^{alaihi salam} was a wise and old man, so he knew that his other sons would not be happy to hear about Yousuf's dream. So, he warned him,

"My son! do not tell any of your brothers about your dream. They will be jealous of you, and they will become your enemies."

Yusuf^{alaihi salam} regarded his father's warning. He did not tell his brothers what he had seen. It is well known that they hate him so much that it was difficult for him to feel secure telling them what was in his heart and in his dreams.

Yusuf^{alaihi salam} was eighteen years old, very handsome and robust, with a gentle temperament. He was respectful, kind, and considerate. His brother Binyamin was equally pleasant. Both were from one mother, Rahel. Because of their refined qualities, the father loved the two more than his other children, and would not let them out of his sight. To protect them, he kept them busy with work in the house garden.

THE PLOT AGAINST YUSUF^{ALAIHI SALAM}

Indeed, Yusuf^{alaihi salam} kept his father's order and did not tell his brothers about his vision. In spite of this, his brothers sat down to conspire against him.

One of them asked: "Why does our father love Yusuf more than us?"

Another answered: "Perhaps because of his beauty."

A third said: "Yusuf and his brother occupied our father's heart."

The first complained: "Our father has gone all astray."

One of them suggested a solution to the matter; "Kill Yusuf!"

"Where should we kill him?"

"We should banish him away from these grounds."

"We will send him to a distant land."

"Why should we not kill him and have rest, so that the favor of your father may be given to you alone?"

However, Judah (Yahudh), the eldest and most intelligent among them, said: "There is no need to kill him when all you want is to get rid of him. Look here, let us throw him into a well and he will be picked up by a passing caravan. They will take him with them to a distant land. He will disappear from your father's sight, and our purpose will be served with his exile. Then after that, we shall repent for our crime and become good people once again."

The discussion continued on the idea of dropping Yusuf[alaihi salam] into a well, as it was seen as the safest solution. They rejected the plan to kill him; kidnap into a distant land was approved. It was the cleverest of ideas.

Then, the ten brothers went to their father and requested him,

"O our father! Why do you not trust us with Yusuf, when we are indeed his well-wishers? Send him with us tomorrow to enjoy himself and play, and verily! we will take care of him."

"Yusuf is our dear little brother," said one of them.

"We are the sons of the same father. So, what are you afraid of? Please send him with us." said another brother.

"We will watch over him."

But Yaqoob[alaihi salam] was terrified for Yusuf[alaihi salam]. He said,

"I fear the wolf may take him while you are playing." He knew that the brothers were jealous of him and that they did not love him. He refused at first.

"Never!" replied a brother. "How can a wolf eat him when we are there? We are strong, and we can save him, father."

After a lot of compulsion from the brothers, Yaqoob[alaihi salam] permitted them to take Yusuf[alaihi salam] along with them.

The next day, they were excited that they could now get rid of Yusuf for after this they could stand a better chance of receiving their father's affection. The brothers took Yusuf[alaihi salam] with them to the forest. They walked through the forest and went directly to the well as they had planned. They leaned over the rail on the pretext of drinking water.

It was then that one of the brothers put his arms around Yusuf[alaihi salam] and held him tightly. Startled by his unusual behavior, Yusuf[alaihi salam] struggled to free himself. Then all the brothers joined and held him so that he could not move. Then, one of them removed his shirt. Together, they lifted Yusuf[alaihi salam] and cast him into the deep well. Young Yusuf's[alaihi salam] piteous pleas made no difference to their cruel hearts. He cried for help and begged his brothers to save him but the brothers shook their heads and paid no heed to the pleas of their brother.

Yusuf[alaihi salam] was all alone in the deep dark well. He was very scared and weeping. Then Allah[subhanahu wa ta'ala] revealed to him that he was safe and should not fear, for he would meet them again someday to remind them of what they had done. The shallow water saved him. He then clung to a rock ledge and climbed on top of it. His brothers left him in this desolate place.

Then they killed a sheep, and soaked Yusuf's shirt in its blood. One brother said that they should swear to keep their deed a close secret. All of them took the oath, and they came weeping to their father in the early part of the night.

"Why this weeping? Has anything happened to our flock?" Yaqoob[alaihi salam] wondered.

They answered crying: "O our father! We went racing with one another and left Yusuf by our belongings and a wolf devoured him; but you will never believe us even when we speak the truth."

"We were surprised after returning from the race that Yusuf was in the wolf's belly."

"We did not see him!"

"You will not believe us even though we are truthful! we are telling you what happened!"

"The wolf has eaten Yusuf!"

"This is Yusuf's shirt. We found it stained with blood and did not find Yusuf!"

They brought his shirt stained with false blood. Deep down in the heart, Yaqoob^alaihi salam knew that his beloved son was still alive and that his other sons were lying. He held the blood-stained shirt in his hands, spread it out and remarked,

"What a merciful wolf! he ate up my beloved son without tearing his shirt!"

The faces of his sons turned red when Yaqoob^alaihi salam demanded more information, but each swore by Allah that they were telling the truth.

"Nay! But your own selves have made up a tale. So, for me, patience is more fitting. It is Allah alone whose help can be sought against that which you assert." The brokenhearted father burst into tears.

The father acted wisely by praying for mighty patience which is free of doubt, and by trusting in Allah for help against what they had plotted against him and his son.

FIRST LADDER TO THE GREATNESS

In the dark well, Yusuf[alaihi salam] managed to find a stone ledge to hold on to. Around him was total darkness and a creepy silence. Fearful thoughts entered his mind,

"What would happen to me?"

"Where would I find food?"

"Why had my own brothers turned against me?"

"Would my father know of my plight?"

His father's smile flashed before him, recalling the love and affection he had always shown him. Yusuf[alaihi salam] began to pray earnestly, pleading to Allah[subhanahu wa ta'ala] for salvation. Gradually, his fear subsided. His Creator was testing the young man with a great misfortune in order to infuse in him a spirit of patience and courage. Yusuf[alaihi salam] submitted himself to the will of his Lord.

A group of people was traveling through that wilderness. At the horizon is a lengthy line of camels, horses, and men; a caravan on its way to Egypt. The caravan of merchants halted at this famous well for water. They were thirsty and looking for water. When they saw the well, they sent a man to bring them some water. The man came to the well and led down a bucket.

Yusuf[alaihi salam] was startled by the bucket hurtling down and grabbed hold of it before it could land in the water. As the man began to haul, he felt the load unusually heavy, so he peeped into the well. What he saw shocked him; a young man was clinging to the rope! He gripped the rope and shouted to his friends,

"Better give me a hand, fellows! Looks like I found a real treasure in the well!"

His companions rushed to the well and helped him to pull out the stranger holding onto the rope. Soon, standing before them was a healthy, handsome youth, beaming with an angelic smile. They saw in him a handsome prize; for money was all that mattered to them. Immediately, they clamped iron shackles on his feet and took him along to Egypt, far away from his beloved homeland of Canaan.

They traveled for many days and nights through the desert. And after many days of travel, they finally arrived in Egypt. The travelers went to the market and put Yusuf^{alaihi salam} for auction. All over the Egyptian city, the news spread that an unusually handsome, robust young slave was on sale. People gathered by the hundreds at the slave market. Some were spectators, others were bidders. The elite and the rich, each one craning his neck to view the handsome specimen. The auctioneer had an amazing day as the bidding went wild, each buyer trying to outbid the other.

"Who will buy this handsome young boy?" They shouted.

Eventually, the Aziz, the chief minister of Egypt, outbid all the others and took Yusuf^{alaihi salam} to his mansion. The chains of slavery have closed on Yusuf^{alaihi salam}. He was cast into the well, deprived of his father, picked from the well, made a slave, sold at the market, and made the property of this man, the Aziz, the chief minister. The hazards followed in quick succession, leaving Yusuf^{alaihi salam} helpless.

What we see as hazards and slander is the first step of the ladder on his way to greatness. Allah^{subhanahu wa ta'ala} is decisive in his action and his plan is carried out despite the plans of others. Allah has promised Yusuf^{alaihi salam} prophethood.

Love for Yusuf^{alaihi salam} was thrust into the heart of the man who bought him, and he was a man of no mean position. He was an important personage, one of the ruling class of Egypt. Therefore, Yusuf^{alaihi salam} was pleasantly surprised when the chief minister of Egypt ordered his men to remove the heavy shackles from his swollen feet. He was also surprised when he told Yusuf^{alaihi salam} not to betray his trust; he would not be ill-treated if he behaved himself. Yusuf^{alaihi salam} smiled at his benefactor, thanked him, and promised to be loyal.

Yusuf^{alaihi salam} felt at ease, for at last he was sheltered and would be well cared for. He thanked Allah^{subhanahu wa ta'ala} over and over, and wondered at the mysterious of life. Not so long ago, he had been cast into a deep, dark well with no hope of ever coming out alive. Next, he was rescued, then enslaved in iron shackles, and now he was moving freely in a luxurious mansion with enough food to enjoy. But his heart ached with longing for his parents and brother Binyamin, and he shed tears daily.

THE SECOND TRIAL OF YUSUF^{ALAIHI SALAM}

Yusuf^{alaihi salam} was made the personal attendant of the chief minister's wife. He was obedient and ever-obliging. With his pleasant manners and charming behavior, he won everybody's heart. His handsomeness became the talk of the town. People referred to him as the most attractive man they had ever seen and wrote poetry about him. His face carried immaculate beauty. The purity of his inner soul and his heart showed in his face, increasing his beauty. People from afar came to the city to have a glimpse of him. The prettiest of maidens and the richest of ladies craved to possess him, but not once did he show arrogance or pride. He was always humble and polite.

Yusuf^{alaihi salam} was given wisdom in affairs and knowledge of life and its conditions. He has given the art of conversation, captivating those who heard him. He was given the nobility and self-restraint, which made him an irresistible personality. His master soon knew that Allah^{subhanahu wa ta'ala} had graced him with Yusuf^{alaihi salam}. He understood that he was the most honest, straightforward, and noble person he had met in his life. So, he put Yusuf^{alaihi salam} in charge of his household, honored him, and treated him as a son.

The wife of the chief minister, Zulaikha, watched Yusuf^{alaihi salam} from day to day. She sat with him, talked with him, listened to him, and her wonder increased over the passage of time.

Yusuf^{alaihi salam} was then confronted with another trial of Allah^{subhanahu wa ta'ala}. Zulaikha now could not resist the handsome Yusuf^{alaihi salam}, and her obsession with him caused her sleepless nights. She fell in love with him, and it was painful for her to be so close to a man, yet be unable to hold him. Yet, she was not a wayward woman, for in her position she could get any man she desired. By all accounts, she must have been a very pretty and intelligent lady, or why would the chief minister have chosen her of all the pretty women in the kingdom? Although she bore him no child, he would not take another wife, as he loved her passionately.

As she could not control her passion any longer. One day, when the Prophet was alone with her in the bedroom, she tried to kiss him. But Yusuf^{alaihi salam} feared Allah^{subhanahu wa ta'ala}, so he denied as he was an upright worshipper of God. He rushed away from her towards the door. Yusuf's^{alaihi salam} refusal only heightened her passion. As he moved towards the door to escape, she ran after him and caught hold of his shirt, like a drowning person clinging to the boat. In her tugging, she tore his shirt and held the torn piece in her hand. They reached the door together. It opened suddenly, there stood her husband and a relative of hers.

Yusuf^{alaihi salam} saw her husband standing in front of him. The sly woman immediately changed her tone to anger and started showing the torn piece of the shirt in her hand. She said to her husband,

"What is the punishment for the one who intended an evil design against your wife? We should put him in prison!"

She was now accusing Yusuf^{alaihi salam} of molesting her, to give the impression that she was innocent and a victim of his desire. However, puzzled Yusuf^{alaihi salam} denied it,

"It was she who wanted to seduce me."

They passed the shirt from hand to hand, while she watched. The witness (her cousin) looked at it and found that it was torn at the back. The evidence showed that she was guilty. The disappointed husband remarked to his wife,

"If he was the one who attacked you, the shirt would have been torn in the front. But his shirt is torn from the back, which means you are lying. Surely, it was your plot!" He retorted.

The wise and just Aziz apologized to Yusuf^{alaihi salam} for his wife's indecency. He also instructed her to beg Yusuf^{alaihi salam} forgiveness for accusing him falsely.

An incident like this cannot remain a secret in a house filled with servants, and the story spread. The news of the incident spread in the town like wildfire. Women began to see Zulaikha's behavior as shocking.

Naturally, their gossip distressed Zulaikha. She honestly believed that it was not easy for any woman to resist a man as handsome as Yusuf^{alaihi salam}. To prove her helplessness, she planned to subject those women to the same temptation she faced. She invited them to a lavish banquet. No one so invited would want to miss the honor of dining with the chief minister's wife; besides, they secretly harbored the desire to meet the handsome Yusuf face to face. Some of her close friends jokingly said they would come only if she introduced them to Yusuf^{alaihi salam}.

The invitation was restricted to ladies. The banquet began, laughter and mirth abounded. Etiquette dictated that the ladies not mention the topic of Yusuf^{alaihi salam}. They were shocked, therefore, when Zulaikha herself opened the topic.

يُوسُف
(*Yūsuf*)

"I have heard of those who say I have fallen in love with the young Hebrew man, Yusuf."

Silence fell upon the banquet. At once, all the guests' hands stopped, and all eyes fell on the chief minister's wife. She said while giving orders for the fruit to be served:

"I admit that he is a charming fellow. I do not deny that I love him. I have loved him for a long time."

The confession of the chief minister's wife removed the tension among the ladies. After finishing their dinner, the guests began cutting their fruit. At that very moment, she summoned Yusuf^{alaihi salam} to make his appearance. He entered the hall gracefully; his gaze was down. Zulaikha called him by his name and he raised his head. The guests were astonished and dumbfounded. His face was shining and full of angelic beauty. It reflected complete innocence, so much that one could feel the peace of mind in the depth of his soul.

They exclaimed in astonishment while continuing to cut the fruit. All their eyes were on Yusuf^{alaihi salam}. The presence of Yusuf^{alaihi salam} was so effective that the women began to cut their palm absent mindedly without feeling any pain.

One of the ladies gasped: "How perfect is Allah!"

Another whispered: "This is not a mortal being!"

Another stammered, patting her hair: "He is a noble angel."

Then the chief minister's wife stood up and announced:

"This is the one for whom they have blamed me. I do not deny that I tempted him. You have been enchanted by Yusuf's single sight and see what has happened to your hands. I have tempted him, and if he does not do what I want of him, I shall imprison him."

"Oh, Lord!" the Prophet calmly replied. "I would rather go to prison than committing a sin. I don't want to be one of those who commit sin and deserve blame, or those who do deeds of the ignorants."

That evening, Zulaikha convinced her husband that the only way to save her honor was to put Yusuf^{alaihi salam} in prison; otherwise, she could not control herself or to safeguard his prestige. The chief minister knew Yusuf^{alaihi salam} was absolutely innocent, that he was a young man of honor, a loyal servant, and he loved him for all these reasons. The chief minister loved him like a son and he had never met anyone who was so loyal to him. It was not an easy decision for him to put an innocent man behind bars. However, he was left with no choice. He reasoned that honor of Yusuf^{alaihi salam} would also be safeguarded if he kept him out of Zulaikha's sight. That night, with a heavy heart, the chief minister sent Yusuf^{alaihi salam} to prison.

THE IMPRISONMENT OF AN INNOCENT

Prison was the third test of Yusuf^{alaihi salam}. During this period, Allah^{subhanahu wa ta'ala} blessed him with an extraordinary gift; the ability to interpret dreams. There were people in the prison who knew that Yusuf^{alaihi salam} was a noble young man, with expert knowledge and a merciful heart. They loved and respected him. At about the same time, two other men landed in the prison. One was the cupbearer of the King; the other was the King's cook. The two men sensed that Yusuf^{alaihi salam} did not look like a criminal, for an aura of piousness glowed on his face. That night, both the new inmates had a strange dream. When they woke up, they were confused as they could not understand the meaning of the dream. They were anxious to have them explained.

The king's cook dreamed that he stood in a place with bread on his head, and two birds were eating the bread. The cupbearer dreamed that he was serving wine to the king. The two went to Yusuf^{alaihi salam} and told him their dreams, asking him to give them their meaning.

On hearing this, Prophet Yusuf^{alaihi salam} first called them to Allah^{subhanahu wa ta'ala}. Then, he told them the meaning of their dreams. He said that the cook would be crucified until he died and birds will eat from his head.

Then Yusuf^{alaihi salam} asked the cupbearer to tell him about his dream.

"I saw that I was standing inside the palace and serving wine to the king."

The Prophet prayed for some time and said,

"You will be soon let free and return to the service of the king." The Prophet then asked the cupbearer to talk to the king about him and tell him that there was a wronged soul named Yusuf in the prison.

What Yusuf^{alaihi salam} predicted did happen; the cook was crucified, and the cupbearer returned to the palace. After the cupbearer returned to service, Satan made him forget to mention Yusuf^{alaihi salam} to the king. Therefore, he remained in prison for a few years, but he was persistent by praying to Allah^{subhanahu wa ta'ala}.

YUSUF'S^{ALAIHI SALAM} INNOCENCE ESTABLISHED

A few years later, one night, the king was sleeping in his palace. He had a strange dream that night. He saw that he was standing at the banks of River Nile. The water was receding, revealing the bare mud. He saw the fish skipping and jumping without water.

Then, he saw seven fat cows emerging from the water, followed by seven lean cows. The lean cows then began swallowing the fat cows. The king was terrified after seeing this.

He then saw seven ears of green corn growing by the riverbank. Suddenly, they disappeared and, in its place, grows seven dry ears of corn.

The king awoke frightened, shocked, and depressed, not knowing what all this meant. He sent servants for the sorcerers, priests, and ministers, to come. He told them his dream.

The sorcerers said: "This is a mixed-up dream. How can any of that be? It is a nightmare."

The priests said: "Perhaps his majesty had a heavy supper."

The Chief Minister said: "Could it be that his majesty was exposed and did not draw the blanket up at night?"

The King's jester said, jokingly: "His majesty is growing old, and so his dreams are confused."

They reached a unanimous conclusion that it was only a nightmare.

The news reached the cupbearer. He remembered the dream he had in prison and compared it to the king's dream, and, therefore Yusuf^alaihi salam came to his mind. He ran to the king to tell him about Yusuf^alaihi salam, who was the only one capable of interpreting the dream.

The cupbearer said: "He had asked me to remember him to you, but I forgot." The king sent the cupbearer to ask Yusuf^alaihi salam about the dream.

Yusuf^alaihi salam interpreted it to him: "There will be seven years of abundance. If the land is properly cultivated, there will be an excess of the good harvest, more than the people will need. This should be stored. Thereafter, seven years of drought will follow in the kingdom. People will not have enough to eat and food will be scarce all over the Egypt, during which they could use the excess grain."

He also advised that during the famine, they should save some grain to be used for seed for the next harvest. Yusuf^alaihi salam then added; "After seven years of drought, there will be a year during which water will be plentiful. If they properly use the water, grapevines and olive trees will grow in abundance, providing plenty of grapes and olive oil."

The cupbearer hurried back with the pleasant news. The interpretation of Yusuf^alaihi salam fascinated the king. He was greatly astonished. Who could this person be? He commanded that Yusuf^alaihi salam be set free from prison and presented to him at once.

The king's envoy went to fetch him immediately, but Yusuf^alaihi salam refused to leave the prison unless his innocence was proven. Perhaps they accused him of cutting the ladies' hands or trying to allure them. Perhaps any other false accusation was made. We do not know exactly what they said to the people to justify Yusuf's^{alaihi salam} sentence to prison.

The envoy returned to the king.

"Where is Yusuf? Did I not command you to fetch him?" The king asked.

The envoy replied: "He refused to leave until his innocence is established regarding the ladies who cut their hands."

The king felt that Yusuf^{alaihi salam} had been harmed unfairly, but he did not exactly know how that happened. So, he immediately ordered an inquiry.

The king ordered: "Bring the wives of the ministers and the wife of the chief minister at once!"

They brought the wife of the chief minister into his court along with the other ministers' wives.

The king asked: "What is the story of Yusuf? What do you know about him? Is it true that he tried to molest the chief minister's wife??"

One of the ladies interrupted the king exclaiming: "Allah forbid!"

A second said: "We know of no evil he has done."

A third said: " He is innocent as the angels."

Now, the eyes of everyone turned to the wife of the chief minister. She now wore a wrinkled face and had lost weight. She had been overwhelmed by sorrow over Yusuf^{alaihi salam} while he was in prison. She boldly confessed that she had lied, and he had told the truth.

"I tempted him, but he refused. He is surely one of the truthful."

She confirmed what she said, not out of fear of the king or the other ladies, but for Yusuf^{alaihi salam} to know that she had never betrayed him during his absence, for he was still in her mind and soul. Of all the creation, he was the only one she loved for, so she confirmed his innocence before all.

Qur'anic verses reflect that she had turned to Prophet's religion, monotheism. His imprisonment was a significant turning point in her life. After this, the story of the chief minister's wife is not mentioned in the Qur'an. We do not know what happened to her after she gave clear evidence. Yet still there are legends about her. Some say that after her husband died, she married Yusuf^{alaihi salam}, and behold she was a virgin. She confessed that her husband had been old and had never touched women. Other legends said that she lost her sight, weeping for Yusuf^{alaihi salam}. She abandoned her palace and wandered in the streets of the city.

"The truth has come and falsehood has vanished. Surely, falsehood is bound to vanish!"

ALLAH ELEVATED YUSUF^{ALAIHI SALAM} TO GLORY

The king informed Yusuf^{alaihi salam} that his innocence was established and ordered him to come to the palace for an interview. The king recognized his noble qualities. When Yusuf^{alaihi salam} came, the king was stunned by this handsome young man. However, the king spoke to him in his tongue. Yusuf's^{alaihi salam} replies astonished the king with his cultural refinement and wide knowledge. He was convinced that Yusuf^{alaihi salam} was very intelligent indeed.

Then the conversation turned to the dream. Yusuf^{alaihi salam} advised the king to start planning for years of famine ahead. He informed him that the famine would affect not only Egypt but the neighboring countries as well. The king offered him an influential position but Yusuf^{alaihi salam} asked to be made the controller of the granaries so he could guard the nation's harvest and thereby safeguard it during the expected drought. By this, Yusuf^{alaihi salam} did not mean to seize an opportunity or personal gain; he merely wanted to rescue hungry nations for a period of seven years. It was a sheer self-sacrifice on his part.

We bestow of Our Mercy on whom We please, and We make not to be lost the reward of Al-Muhsinen (the doers of good)". [Surah Yusuf: 56]

The wheels of time turned, Yusuf[alaihi salam] had now become one of the senior-most officials in Egypt. During the seven wonderful years, Yusuf[alaihi salam] had full control over the cultivation, harvesting, and storage of crops. He did his duties faithfully and managed to carefully save the grains for the harsh years ahead.

Then, as the Prophet Yusuf[alaihi salam] had predicted, drought followed and famine spread throughout the region, including Canaan, the homeland of Yusuf[alaihi salam]. The leaves turned yellow, and not even a single drop of rain fell from the sky. But nobody in Egypt died of hunger because the Prophet had saved more than enough grains for the harsh years.

"You were right, Yusuf." the king said to the Prophet. "It's only because of you that our people are not suffering. But all of our neighbors are asking for our help. What should I tell them?" He asked.

"Allah[subhanahu wa ta'ala] saved us." The Prophet replied, "We are blessed to have plenty of grains with us. I think this is the time we should help our neighbors. We should sell the grains to the needy nations at a fair price. In this way, we can save many lives."

The king agreed and the delightful news spread all over the region.

As this famine affected Canaan as well. Prophet Yaqoob[alaihi salam] sent ten of his sons, all except Binyamin, to Egypt to purchase provisions. The brothers traveled for many days and finally arrived in Egypt.

Yusuf[alaihi salam] heard of the ten brothers who had come from afar and who could not speak the language of the Egyptians. When they called on him to purchase their needs, Yusuf[alaihi salam] immediately recognized his brothers, but they did not recognize him. How could they? To them, Yusuf[alaihi salam] no longer existed; they had thrown him into the deep, dark well many years ago!

Yusuf[alaihi salam] received them warmly. After supplying them with provisions, he asked where they had come from.

They explained: "We came from Canaan. We are eleven brothers, the children of a noble Prophet. The youngest is at home tending to the needs of our aging father."

On hearing this, Yusuf's[alaihi salam] eyes filled with tears; his longing for home swelled up in his heart, as well as his longing for his beloved parents and his loving brother Binyamin.

"Are you truthful people?" Yusuf[alaihi salam] asked them.

Perturbed they replied, "What reasons do we have to lie to you?"

"If what you say is true, then bring your brother as proof and I will reward you with double rations. But if you do not bring him to me, it would be better if you do not return," Yusuf[alaihi salam] warned them.

They assured him that they would gladly fulfill his command but that they would have to get their father's permission. As an inducement to return with their brother, Yusuf[alaihi salam] ordered his servant to secretly place the bag of money they had paid, into one of their grain sacks.

After many days of travel, they reached Canaan. Before they could unload the camels, they greeted their father, then criticized him: "They denied us some supplies because you did not let your son go with us. They would not give us food for absentees. Why would you not entrust him with us? Please, send him with us, and we shall take care of him."

Prophet Yaqoob^{alaihi salam} became sad and told them: "I will not permit Binyamin to travel with you. I will not part with him, for I entrusted Yusuf to you and you failed me."

Later, when they opened their grain sacks, they were surprised to find the money bag returned intact. They rushed to their father;

"Look, father! The noble official has returned our money; this is surely proof that he would not harm our brother and it can only benefit us." But Yaqoob^{alaihi salam} refused to send Binyamin with them.

After some time, when they had no more grain, Yaqoob^{alaihi salam} asked them to travel to Egypt for more. They reminded him of the warning the Egyptian official had given them. They could not return without Binyamin.

"I will not send him with you unless you give me a pledge in Allah's name that you shall bring him back to me as safely as you take him."

So, they gave their sincere pledge.

Yaqoob^{alaihi salam} reminded them: " Allah^{subhanahu wa ta'ala} is witness to your pledge."

He agreed, then advised them to enter the city through several different gates. Yaqoob^{alaihi salam} blessed them on their departure and prayed to Allah for their protection. The brothers undertook the lengthy journey to Egypt, taking good care of Binyamin.

THE INTERPRETATION OF THE DREAM IN REALITY

When they arrived in Egypt, Yusuf^{alaihi salam} welcomed them heartily and he suppressed the desire to embrace Binyamin that arose within him. He prepared a feast for them and seated them in pairs. Yusuf^{alaihi salam} arranged to sit next to his beloved brother Binyamin, who began to weep.

"Why are you crying?" Yusuf^{alaihi salam} asked him.

He replied: "If my brother Yusuf had been here, I would have sat next to him."

That night, when Yusuf^{alaihi salam} and Binyamin were alone in a room, Yusuf^{alaihi salam} asked his brother,

"Would you like to have me as your brother?"

Binyamin respectfully answered that he regarded his host as a wonderful person, but he could never take the place of his brother.

Yusuf^{alaihi salam} broke down, and amidst flowing tears said; "My loving brother, I am your brother who was lost and whose name you are constantly repeating. Fate has brought us together after many years of separation. This is Allah's favor. But let it be a secret between us for the time being." Binyamin flung his arms around Yusuf^{alaihi salam} and both brothers shed tears of joy.

The next day, while their bags were being filled with grains to load onto the camels, Yusuf^{alaihi salam} ordered one of his assistants to place the king's golden measuring cup into Binyamin's saddlebag. When the brothers were ready to set out, the soldiers came running to them. The gates were locked, and a soldier shouted,

"O you travelers, stop there! you are thieves!"

The accusation was most unusual, and the people gathered around them.

"What have you lost?" his brothers inquired.

"The king's golden cup. Whoever can trace it, we will give a beast load of grain." a soldier said.

The brothers said with all innocence: "We have not come here to corrupt the land and steal."

One of the soldiers said (as Yusuf^{alaihi salam} had instructed them): "What punishment should you choose for the thief?"

The brothers answered: "According to our law, whoever steals becomes a slave to the owner of the property."

The officers agreed: "Then we shall apply your law instead of the Egyptian law, which states for imprisonment."

The chief officer ordered his soldiers to start searching the caravan. Yusuf^{alaihi salam} was watching the incident from high upon his throne. He had given instructions for Binyamin's bag to be the last one to be searched. When they did not find the cup in the bags of the ten older brothers, the brothers sighed in relief. There remained only the bag of their youngest brother.

Yusuf^{alaihi salam} said, intervening for the first time, "There was no need to search his saddle as he did not look like a thief."

"We will not move an inch unless his saddle is searched as well. We are the sons of a nobleman, not thieves." his brothers affirmed.

The soldiers reached in their bags and pulled out the king's cup. The brothers exclaimed,

"If he steals now, a brother of his has stolen before." They strayed from the present issue in order to blame a particular group of the children of Yaqoob^{alaihi salam}.

Prophet Yusuf^{alaihi salam} heard their hatred with his own ears and was filled with regret. Yet, he swallowed his anger, keeping it within. He said to himself, "You went further and did worse; it shall go bad with you and worse hereafter, and Allah knows your intention."

Silence fell upon them after these remarks by the brothers. Then they forgot their secret satisfaction and thought of Prophet Yaqoob^{alaihi salam}; they had taken an oath with him that they would not betray his son. They began to beg Yusuf^{alaihi salam} for mercy.

"Yusuf, O minister! Take one of us instead. O ruler of the land! Verily, he has an old father who will grieve for him. He is the son of a good man, and we can see you are an honorable man too."

Yusuf[alaihi salam] answered calmly: "How can you want to set free the man who has stolen the king's cup? It would be sinful."

The brothers went on pleading for mercy. However, the guards said that the king had spoken and his word was law.

So, when they despaired of him, they held a conference in private. Judah, the eldest, was much worried and told the others,

"We promised our father in the name of Allah not to fail him. I will, therefore, stay behind and will only return if my father permits me to do so."

The brothers left enough provisions behind for Judah, who stayed at a tavern awaiting the fate of Binyamin. In the meantime, Yusuf[alaihi salam] kept Binyamin in his house as his personal guest and told him how he had devised the plot to put the king's cup in his bag, in order to keep him behind, so as to protect him. He was also glad that Judah had stayed behind, as he was a good-hearted brother. Yusuf[alaihi salam] secretly arranged to watch over Judah's wellbeing.

Yusuf's[alaihi salam] plan in sending the others back, was to test their sincerity. To see if they would come back for the two brothers they had left behind.

When they arrived home, they entered upon their father calling,

"O our father! Your son has stolen!"

Prophet Yaqoob[alaihi salam] was puzzled, scarcely believing the news. Then, the brothers told him everything. He was overwhelmed with sorrow and his eyes wept tears.

"Patience be with me; perhaps Allah^subhanahu wa ta'ala will return all of them to me. He is Most Knowing, Most Wise."

Solitude surrounded him, yet he found consolation in patience and trusted in Allah. He was deeply hurt. Only prayer could comfort him and strengthen his faith and patience. Weeping all those years for his beloved son Yusuf^alaihi salam; and now one more of his best son had been snatched from him. Yaqoob^alaihi salam almost lost his sight weeping on this loss.

The other sons pleaded with him: "O father, you are a noble prophet and a great messenger of Allah. Revelations descended on you, and people received guidance and faith from you. Why are you destroying yourself in this way?"

He replied: "Rebuking me will not lessen my grief. Only the return of my sons will comfort me. My sons, go in search of Yusuf and his brother; do not despair of Allah's mercy."

Allah, the Almighty told us: They said: "By Allah! You will never cease remembering Yusuf until you become weak with old age, or until you be of the dead."

He said: "I only complain of my grief and sorrow to Allah, and I know from Allah what you do not know."

Prophet Yaqoob^alaihi salam asked his sons to go to Egypt once again. The caravan set out for Egypt. The brothers - on their way to see the chief minister (Prophet Yusuf^alaihi salam) - were became poor and depressed.

In the end, they pleaded Yusuf^{alaihi salam}. They asked charities of him, appealing to his heart, reminding him that Allah rewards charity givers. At this moment, in the midst of their plight, Prophet Yusuf^{alaihi salam} spoke to them in their native tongue.

"Do you know what you did with Yusuf and his brother when you were ignorant?"

The brothers were shocked by listening to this. As they knew that this secret is only known to them and Yusuf^{alaihi salam}.

They said: "Are you our brother Yusuf?"

He said: "I am Yusuf. And Binyamin is my brother. Allah has indeed been Gracious to us. Whoever fears Allah and is patient, then surely, Allah always rewards them."

The brothers trembled with fear.

"We have sinned, Brother. Allah has certainly preferred you above us." They said.

But Yusuf^{alaihi salam} comforted them. "No reproach on you this day. May Allah forgive you, and He is the Most Merciful of those who show mercy."

Yusuf^{alaihi salam} embraced them, and they wept together with joy. Yusuf^{alaihi salam} couldn't leave his responsible office without proper replacement, so he advised his brothers. "Go with this shirt of mine, and caress it over the face of my father, he will recover his sight. And bring to me all of your family."

The brothers agreed and left for Canaan. As they approached near the Canaan, Prophet Yaqoob^{alaihi salam} sensed the scent of Yusuf^{alaihi salam} in the air. He stood up all of a sudden, got dressed and went to meet his sons.

The wife of the eldest son remarked: " Yaqoob^{alaihi salam} has come out of his room today." The women inquired about what was wrong. There was a hint of a smile on his face.

The others asked him: "How do you feel today?"

He answered: "I can smell Yusuf in the air."

The wives left him alone, saying to one another that there was no hope for him. "He will die of weeping over Yusuf."

"Did he talk about Yusuf's shirt?"

"I do not know. He said he could smell him; perhaps he has gone mad."

That night, the old man wanted a cup of milk to break his fast, for he had been fasting. As the caravan approached nearer, the Prophet kept praying to Allah^{subhanahu wa ta'ala}. When the caravan finally arrived, Prophet Yaqoob^{alaihi salam} came outside and asked, "I do indeed feel the smell of Yusuf. Is it real?"

"You are certainly mistaken." Said one wife.

But the Prophet was indeed telling the truth. The bearer of the glad tidings arrived. One of his sons caress the shirt over his face, and Yaqoob^{alaihi salam} became clear-sighted.

"Did I not tell you that I know from Allah that you don't know." He said to them happily.

The brothers had realized their mistakes. They asked Prophet Yaqoob^{alaihi salam},

"We have sinned, Father. Ask Forgiveness from Allah for our sins."

He said: "I will ask my Lord for forgiveness for you, verily, He! Only He is the Oft-Forgiving, the Most Merciful."

Then, Prophet Yaqoob^{alaihi salam} left for Egypt to meet his son. Prophet Yusuf^{alaihi salam} received him with great joy. He placed his father on his throne. Yaqoob's^{alaihi salam} happiness knew no bound. Then his parents and all the eleven brothers prostrated before Prophet Yusuf^{alaihi salam}.

"This is the dream that I saw when I was young. I saw eleven stars, the sun, and the moon, bowing down to me. My Lord has made it come true."

Prophet Yusuf^{alaihi salam} arranged an audience with the king for himself and his family, to ask the king's permission for them to settle in Egypt. He was an asset to the kingdom, and the king was happy to have him stay with his household. He then prostrated to Allah^{subhanahu wa ta'ala} in gratitude. This dominant power and responsibility did not distract the Prophet from Allah. He remembered his creator and benefactor all the time.

Prophet Yusuf^{alaihi salam} did not want to die the death of a king. He didn't like to be gathered around the people of royalty. He wanted to die the death of a slave to Allah and to be gathered around the righteous people. At the time of his death, he asked his brothers to bury him beside his forefathers. So, when he passed away, he was mummified and placed in a coffin until a suitable time to be taken out of Egypt. It is said that he died at the age of one hundred and ten.

Therefore, it was narrated that Allah's Messenger Muhammad (PBUH) was asked: "Who is the most honorable amongst the people?" He replied: "The most God-fearing." The people said: "We do not want to ask you about this." He said: "The most honorable person is Yusuf, Allah's prophet, the son of Allah's prophet, the son of the faithful friend of Allah (i.e. Ibrahim)." (Sahih Al-Bukhari)

PROPHET

YUNUS

PROPHET YUNUS

(ALAIHI SALAM)

The Owner of the Fish

A long long time ago, there was a city named 'Nineveh'. It was situated on the right bank of the River Tigris in ancient Assyria, across the river from the modern-day major city of Mosul, Iraq. The people of Nineveh were idolaters living a shameless life. Prophet Yunus (Jonah)^{alaihi salam} was sent by Allah^{subhanahu wa ta'ala} to Nineveh to preach to them about the true God.

"You should believe only in Allah^{subhanahu wa ta'ala} and obey his commands." he warned them, "Otherwise a severe punishment will come upon you."

But the inhabitants of the town did not like anyone to interfere in their way of worship.

"We and our forefathers have worshipped these gods for many years." said an old man, "And no harm has come to us."

Prophet Yunus^{alaihi salam} tried very hard to convince the people about Allah^{subhanahu wa ta'ala}, but the people kept ignoring him. He warned that if they kept on with their foolishness, Allah will soon punish them.

Instead of fearing Allah, they told the prophet that they were not afraid of his threats.

"Let your God punish us!" They told him.

The Prophet became disheartened, "In that case, I will leave you to your misery." Saying that he left the town of Nineveh. He became impatient and departed without waiting for further commands from Allah. He knew that God must be angry at him. So, he decided to travel to a distant land.

As soon as the Prophet left the city, the skies began to change its color. It looked like it was on fire. The people were filled by fear at the sight. They remembered the destruction of the people of A'ad, Thamud, and Nuh. Slowly, faith started penetrating their hearts.

They gathered on the top of a mountain and started to pray to Allah for his mercy. The mountains echoed with their cries. The people of Nineveh repented sincerely for the sins they had committed. When Allah heard their prayers, he decided not to punish them. He showered his blessing upon the people once again. When the people realized that they were saved, they prayed to Allah for the return of Prophet Yunus^{alaihi salam}, so that he could guide them.

Meanwhile, Prophet Yunus^{alaihi salam} had boarded a small ship in the company of other passengers. It sailed all day in calm waters, with a good wind blowing at the sails. But as the night came, the sea suddenly changed. There was a horrible storm, and it looked like the ship would be split into pieces. The waves rose as high as mountains, tossing the ship up and down.

Everyone on the ship was terrified. The captain of the ship shouted to the crew to lighten the ship's heavy load. The crew first threw their baggage overboard but this was not enough. Their safety was dependent in reducing the weight further. So, they decided among themselves that one among them will have to be thrown into the sea.

In the meantime, an enormous whale had surfaced behind the ship. Allah^{subhanahu wa ta'ala} had commanded the whale to surface. The whale kept following the ship as he had been commanded.

The captain of the ship told the crew, "We will make lots with all travelers' names. The one whose name is drawn will be thrown into the sea."

Yunus^{alaihi salam} reluctantly took part in the sortition, and his name was added as well. When the lot was drawn, the paper had 'Yunus' written on it. Since the crew knew that the Prophet was the most honorable man among them, they did not want to throw him into the sea. Therefore, they drew a second lot.

When they did the lot for the second time, the name of the Prophet appeared again. The crew decided to try one final time and drew a third lot. But the Prophet's name appeared during the third and final lot as well. Prophet Yunus^{alaihi salam} realized that Allah^{subhanahu wa ta'ala} special will was involved in what was going on. He realized that Allah was testing him because he had abandoned the mission without Allah's consent.

It was decided that the Prophet Yunus^{alaihi salam} should throw himself into the water. Yunus^{alaihi salam} stood at the edge of the ship, looking at the furious sea. It was night and there was no moon in the sky. The stars were hidden behind a black fog. Before jumping into the sea, the Prophet kept mentioning Allah's name. He then jumped into the sea and disappeared beneath the vast waves.

The whale that was following the ship, found the Prophet Yunus^{alaihi salam} floating on the waves. It didn't waste any time and swallowed him in one gulp. The whale shut its ivory teeth as if they were white bolts locking the door of his prison. It then dived to the bottom of the sea. The Prophet imagined himself to be dead, but his senses became alert when he figured that he could move. He realized that he was alive and imprisoned.

In his loneliness, he started to think over what had happened in the town and realized that he should have never left the town. Instead, he should have stayed and kept on speaking to the people, asking them to return to Allah^{subhanahu wa ta'ala}. In his despair, the Prophet prayed with all his heart to Allah.

"O Allah! there is no God apart from you. You alone do I praise and honor. I have done wrong, if you do not help me, I shall be lost forever."

The Prophet continued praying to Allah, repeating his prayers. Fishes, whales and many other creatures that lived in the sea, heard the voice of the Prophet's prayers coming from the whale's stomach. All these creatures gathered around the whale and praised Allah^{subhanahu wa ta'ala}, each in its own language. The whale also participated in praising Allah. Then he understood that he had swallowed a Prophet. The whale felt afraid at first, then said to himself, "Why should I be afraid? Allah commanded me to swallow him."

Allah Almighty saw the sincere repentance of the Prophet Yunus^{alaihi salam} and he decided to save him. He commanded the whale to go to the surface and eject the Prophet onto the shore. The whale obeyed and swam to the surface of the ocean. He then ejected the Prophet Yunus^{alaihi salam} on to a remote island.

The Prophet was very sick now because of the acids inside the whale's stomach. His skin was inflamed, and when the sun rose, the rays burned his body. The Prophet was on the verge of screaming with pain by now, but he endured the pain and continued his prayers to Allah. Allah^{subhanahu wa ta'ala} then caused a tree to grow behind where the Prophet Yunus^{alaihi salam} was praying.

This tree protected the Prophet from the harsh rays of the sun and gave him nourishing fruits as well. Gradually, he regained his strength and found his way back to Nineveh.

He was pleasantly surprised to notice the change that took place. The entire population of Nineveh turned out to welcome him. They informed him that now they worship Allah, the one true God. The Prophet was thrilled to hear that and lived happily until he passed away.

PROPHET MUSA
(ALAIHI SALAM)

An Era of Magic & The Sea Piercer

مُوسَىٰ
(Mūsā)

Prophet Musa^{alaihi-salam} is considered a prophet, a messenger and a leader in Islam. He is the most frequently mentioned individual in the Quran. The Quran states that Prophet Musa^{alaihi-salam} was sent by Allah^{subhanahu wa ta'ala} to the Pharaoh of Egypt and Israelites for guidance and warning.

Prophet Musa^{alaihi-salam} grew up as the prince. The Pharaohs who ruled over Egypt were very cruel towards the descendants of Prophet Yaqoob^{alaihi-salam}. These descendants were known as 'the children of Israel'.

PHARAOH'S DREAM & THE BIRTH OF
MUSA^{ALAIHI-SALAM}

They were kept as slaves and forced to work for small wages, and sometimes even for nothing. The Pharaoh wanted the Israelites to obey only him and worship only his gods. This way many dynasties came to Egypt, and they assumed that they were gods or their representative spokesman. Years passed, and a very cruel man named Phir'oun was the Pharaoh now. He hated the Israelites very much. He punished those Israelites at every given opportunity. He hated to see them multiplying and prospering in his kingdom. One night, when the Pharaoh was sleeping, he had a dream. In his dream, he saw that a huge ball of fire came from the sky and burned down the city. The fire burned the houses of all Egyptians, but the houses of Israelites stayed unharmed. It horrified the Pharaoh. He didn't understand what the dream meant. So, the next day, he called his priests and magicians. He asked them about the dream he had.

The priest said to him, "This means that a boy will be born to the Israelites very soon. Egyptians will perish at the hands of this boy."

The Pharaoh got furious. He ordered to kill every male child born to the Israelites. Pharaoh's order was carried out, and the soldiers began to kill every male child born to the Israelites. It was during at that time that Prophet Musa^{alaihi-salam} was born. The Prophet was born to a poor Israelite family, and he had an elder brother named Haroon^{alaihi-salam}, and a sister too. Allah^{subhanahu wa ta'ala} had a plan for the prophet. He ordered his mother to place him in a basket and allow it to float downstream in the great Nile River.

His mother did as she was told, and she let him float in the river. Her heart grieved for her son. But, she knew that Allah^{subhanahu wa ta'ala} cared for her son, and she knew that no harm will come to him. As the basket floated away, she asked her daughter to follow the basket downstream, and make sure that no harm came to her son. The basket floated in the river for a long time, and the Prophet's sister followed the basket as her mother had instructed.

Allah^{subhanahu wa ta'ala} was guiding the basket and after floating on River Nile for some time, the basket entered a small stream. The Pharaoh's wife was bathing in that stream, and when she saw the basket, she asked her servants to bring it ashore. When she saw the baby, she just fell in love with him. Pharaoh's wife was very different from the Pharaoh. She was a believer, and she was also merciful. She was longing for a child, so when she saw the baby, she hugged and kissed him. It surprised Pharaoh when he saw his wife hugging and kissing the baby. He was astonished as he saw her weeping with the joy which he had never seen before.

"Let me keep this baby, and let him be a son to us." she requested her husband.

The Pharaoh could not refuse her, and they decided to adopt the baby. After some time, the baby started getting hungry and started crying. The Queen summoned a few wet nurses to feed the baby, but he refused to take any of their breast milk. It was then the soldiers brought the sister to the Queen.

"This girl was following the basket." they told her.

Then the sister replied, "I was just following the basket out of curiosity, your highness."

When she saw her brother crying, it worried her. She blurted out.

"I know someone who can feed him." the Queen agreed, and she ordered the soldiers to fetch the woman that the little girl was talking about. The Prophet's sister then brought the mother, and she started to feed him. As the child was put to her breast, he at once started suckling the milk. The Pharaoh who was watching all this was astonished and asked, "Who are you? This child has refused to take any other breast but yours."

The mother of the Prophet knew that if she told them the truth, they would kill them immediately. So, she told them, "I am a woman of sweet milk and sweet smell. That's why no child refuses me." Her answer satisfied the Pharaoh, and they appointed her as his nurse.

TRIAL FROM THE PRINCE OF EGYPT TO MIDIAN'S HARD WORKER

Musa^alaihi-salam grew up in the palace as a prince. Allah granted him good health, strength, knowledge, and wisdom. He had a kind heart, so the weak and oppressed often turned to him seeking help. One day, while he was walking in the city, he saw an Egyptian soldier beating an Israelite. When the Israelite saw the prophet, he begged him for his help. The Prophet decided to help the poor man and asked the soldier to stop beating the Israelite. The soldier questioned his authority and said something that angered the prophet. The Prophet first tried to reason with the soldier but he was not willing to listen. Then the prophet stepped forward and hit the soldier with such a powerful blow that he collapsed and died. When he realized what he had done, a cold sweat broke out from his forehead.

He said to himself, "This is the evil work of Shaitaan. He misled me."

The Prophet knew that it was a sin to kill anyone until he is brought to trial and found guilty. He kneeled on the ground and prayed to Allah,

"O my Lord! I have indeed wronged my soul. Please forgive me."

The next day, he saw the same Israelite fighting with another man. The Prophet helped the weaker ones, and said, "You seem to be involved in fights every day with one or the other."

موسَىٰ
(Mūsā)

The Israelite got scared and said, "I'm so sorry. Please don't kill me like how you killed a soldier yesterday."

The Egyptian with whom the Israelite was fighting, overheard the remarks, and he reported this to the authorities. The next day, when Musa^{alaihi-salam} was walking in the city, a man came running to him.

"Musa! the soldiers are coming to arrest you. Getaway while there is still time." said the man.

The Prophet knew that the penalty for killing an Egyptian was death, so he decided to leave Egypt. The Prophet left Egypt in a hurry. He didn't even bother to change his clothes. He was not prepared for traveling so he didn't have an animal to ride, nor did he have a caravan. He had left as soon as the man warned him.

Prophet Musa^{alaihi-salam} wandered in the desert for many days and nights. He traveled in the direction of 'Midian', which was the nearest town between Syria and Egypt. His only companion in the desert was Allah, and his only provision was piety. The scorching sand burned the soles of his feet, but fearing pursuit by the soldiers, he forced himself to keep walking. He walked for eight days and nights in this condition. The Prophet finally managed to cross the desert, and he reached the outskirts of Midian. After walking for some more time, he reached a watering hole outside the city. As soon as he reached the spring, he threw himself under a tree to rest for some time. As he caught his breath, he noticed two women standing aside with their sheep. They were standing far away, hesitant to approach the crowd. The Prophet sensed that the woman needed help. So being a man of honor, he ignored his thrust and went to them.

"Can I help you in any way? Why are you standing aside?" he asked them.

Then the older sister replied, "We are waiting until the men finish watering their sheep."

"Why are you waiting?" he asked them again.

"We are helpless." they said.

"Our father is very old, and he does not have the strength to face this crowd. If we go forward, these strong men will push us aside. So, when these people are finished, then we take our animals to the water. It's our daily routine." they explained.

The Prophet took the women's sheep to the waterhole where he easily pushed in amongst the men. When he approached the water, he saw that the shepherds had put the large rock to cover the well. The Prophet single-handedly lifted the rock and he let the animals drink. The people standing there were awestruck when they saw him lifting the stone with just one hand. He then returned to sit in the tree's shade. That's when he realized that he had forgotten to drink.

"O Lord!" he prayed, "Whatever good you can bestow on me, I am surely in need of it now."

When their daughters returned home earlier than usual, it surprised their father. The daughters then explained what happened at the Oasis, and why they reached early. Their father wanted to thank the stranger, so he sent one of his daughters to invite the stranger to his home. One of the daughters returned to the prophet and told him, "My father wants to reward you for your kindness, and he invites you to our home." He agreed and accompanied the maiden to her father.

When they reached the house, the Prophet introduced himself and told him the story of his life. He then told them why he had to flee from Egypt. The old man comforted him, "Be grateful to Allah that you have managed to escape from those tyrants. You need not be afraid now."

The old man and his daughters really liked the gentle behavior of the prophet. They invited him to stay with them for a few days, and the prophet was more than happy to accept their invitation. The host soon realized that the prophet was a trustworthy man.

One day, the old man approached him and said, "I wish to marry you to one of my daughters."

The Prophet was happy to hear this.

"But on one condition," the old man added. "You must agree to work for me for a period of eight years."

The Prophet Musa^{alaihi-salam} was a stranger in a strange land. Exhausted and alone, this offer suited him very much. He married the Midianite's daughter and looked after his animals for ten long years. Time passed, and he stayed far away from his family and his people. This period of ten years was very important for the prophet. It was a time for major preparation. Musa^{alaihi-salam} completed ten years of his service as he had promised.

MOUNT TUR & THE REVELATION FROM ALLAH

One day, suddenly he was overcome by homesickness. He started missing his family and the land of Egypt. He desperately wanted to return to Egypt. That night, he went to his wife and said, "We shall leave for Egypt tomorrow."

His wife agreed, and they started packing their belongings. Musa[alaihi-salam] left Midian with his family and traveled through the desert. They traveled for many days and finally reached near Mount Sinai.

"I think we have lost our way." said the Prophet.

Musa[alaihi-salam] was unsure, so he decided to camp there for the night. He then left searching for firewood to light up a fire. He kept searching and reached mount Tur. As he walked, he noticed a fire burning on the top of the mountain. Musa[alaihi-salam] walked towards the fire, and as he did, he heard a voice.

"O Musa! I am Allah, the Lord of the Universe." said the voice.

The Prophet Musa[alaihi-salam] realized that it was indeed God talking to him, and so he walked towards the fire. Allah[subhanahu wa ta'ala] then asked the prophet to remove his shoes as he was standing on a holy ground. God then revealed to him that he had been chosen for a special mission and asked him to follow his instructions.

"And what is it in your right hand?" Allah asked him.

"This is my staff," he replied. "On which I lean, and with which I beat down the branches for my sheep."

"Throw down your staff!" the voice commanded. And no sooner did the Prophet throw down the staff that it turned into a wriggling snake. Musa^{alaihi-salam} was so frightened that he started to run.

But the voice said, "Fear not and grasp your stick, we shall return it to its former state."

The Prophet was terrified of the snake. He then trusted the voice and placed his hand over the snake. It immediately transformed back into a staff again.

The fear of Musa^{alaihi-salam} subsided and was replaced by peace, as he realized that he was indeed talking to God. Next, Allah^{subhanahu wa ta'ala} commanded him to put his hand inside the robe. The Prophet did as commanded, and when he pulled his hand out, it was shining brilliantly.

Allah then commanded him to go to Egypt and face the Pharaoh. He told him that the Pharaoh had become arrogant and was suppressing the Israelites. Musa^{alaihi-salam} feared that he would be arrested if he returned to Egypt. So, he said, "Oh Allah! I have killed a man among them, and I fear they will kill me."

Then Allah^{subhanahu wa ta'ala} comforted him by saying, "Go and deliver this message to them. Show them the path of the truth. Take your brother Haroon, to assist you. They will not be able to harm you at all."

Allah^{subhanahu wa ta'ala} assured him of his safety and the prophet was convinced.

مُوسَىٰ
(Mūsā)

BROTHERS' REUNION & THE FIRST CHALLENGE TO PHARAOH'S ARROGANCE

The Prophet then took his family and set off toward Egypt. They walked for many days, and finally, they arrived in Egypt. When they reached outside the city, his brother Haroon^alaihi-salam was waiting for him. Haroon^alaihi-salam was a prophet as well. He had received the vision from God, and in the vision, he had seen that his younger brother would soon arrive to set the Israelites free. When Musa^alaihi-salam realized that this was his brother, he was in tears. Then both of them walked toward the palace. The prophet had not been to Egypt for many years, and he knew that his life was in danger. Nothing could have brought him back except the command of Allah^subhanahu wa ta'ala.

The prophet could still hear the words of Allah ringing in his ears, "Go to the pharaoh and tell him to let the Israelites leave the land of Egypt."

Musa^alaihi-salam now stood in front of the Pharaoh along with his brother. The Prophet spoke to the Pharaoh about Allah^subhanahu wa ta'ala and his mercy. But the Pharaoh refused to listen because he considered himself as a god. He listened to the Prophet's speech with disdain. He thought the prophet was crazy to question his supreme position. After the Prophet finished delivering Allah's message, the Pharaoh raised his hand and asked, "What do you want?"

"I want you to send the children of Israel with us." answered the Prophet.

"The Israelites are my slaves. Why should I send them with you?"

"They are not your slaves! they are the slaves of Allah." Musa replied.

This answer angered the Pharaoh. "Are you not Musa?"

The Prophet shook his head and answered, "Yes."

"We picked you up from River Nile, and brought you up, didn't we?" asked the Pharaoh. "Are you not Musa who killed an Egyptian man? You are a fugitive of justice, and how dare you come and speak to me?"

The Prophet ignored his sarcasm and explained that he killed the Egyptian in an accident. It was never deliberate. He then informed the pharaoh that Allah[subhanahu wa ta'ala] had granted him forgiveness and that he was now one of his messengers.

The Pharaoh asked Musa[alaihi-salam] to show a sign to prove that he was the messenger of God. The Prophet threw his stick to the floor. It turned into a serpent, slithering and sliding along the floor. The Pharaoh was terrified at first, but he tried hard not to show it.

"Ha!" said the Pharaoh arrogantly.

"We have many sorcerers in our kingdom who can match your magic."

He addressed his advisors: "These are two wizards who will strip you of your best traditions and drive you out of the country with their magic. What do you recommend?"

They advisors said to Pharaoh to detain Musa[alaihi-salam] and his brother while they summoned the cleverest magicians in the country. Then they too, could show their skills of magic and change sticks into serpents. In this way they sought to reduce the influence of his miracles on the masses. The Pharaoh detained the Prophet and his brother at the palace. He then summoned all the best magicians in his kingdom to the palace. The Pharaoh promised huge rewards to them if their magic was found better than the Prophet's.

On the customary festival day, which attracted citizens from all over the Egyptian empire, Pharaoh arranged for a public contest between Musa^{alaihi-salam} and the magicians. The people came in droves as near before when they heard of the greatest contest ever between Pharaoh's many magicians and a single man who claimed to be a Prophet. They had also heard of a baby who had once floated down the river Nile in a basket, landed on Pharaoh's palace grounds, been reared as a prince, and who later had fled for killing an Egyptian with a single blow.

CONTEST BETWEEN MUSA^{ALAIHI-SALAM} & THE MAGICIANS OF EGYPT

The day for the contest arrived, and the palace was crowded with people. The magicians stood on one side, and the Prophet Musa^{alaihi-salam} and his brother Haroon^{alaihi-salam} stood opposite to them. Everyone in the palace took the side of the Pharaoh, and the Prophet and his brother stood alone.

Everyone was eager and excited to watch this great contest. Before it began, Musa^{alaihi-salam} arose. There was a hush in the enormous crowd. Musa^{alaihi-salam} addressed the magicians.

"Grief unto you, if you invent a lie against Allah by calling His miracles magic and by not being honest with the Pharaoh. Woe unto you, if you do not know the difference between the truth and falsehood. Allah will destroy you with His punishment, for he who lies against Allah fails miserably."

Musa^{alaihi-salam} had spoken sincerely and made the magicians think. But they were overwhelmed by their greed for money and glory. They hoped to impress the people with their magic and to expose Musa^{alaihi-salam} as a fraud and a cheat.

Musa^{alaihi-salam} asked the magicians to perform first. It is said that there were over seventy magicians lined up in a row. The magicians threw their sticks and robes, and suddenly the floor was flooded with a sea of serpents.

They were writhing and slithering everywhere. Pharaoh and his men applauded loudly. It amazed the crowd when they saw this, and they thought the Prophet was never going to beat such powerful magic.

Musa^{alaihi-salam} was afraid too, but he knew that Allah was on his side. The Prophet threw his stick to the floor, and suddenly it transformed into a gigantic serpent. The people stood up, craning their necks for a better view. Pharaoh and his men sat silently as one by one the serpent ate all other small ones lying on the ground. Musa^{alaihi-salam} bent to pick it up, and it became a staff in his hand.

When the crowd saw this, they stood up like a wave cheering for the Prophet. A wonder like this had never been seen before. The magicians were surprised and they knew that this was not just a trick and that the serpent was real. They realized that Musa^{alaihi-salam} was not a magician or a sorcerer and his power came from something greater. So, they fell on their knees seeking forgiveness from Allah. Allah forgave them but the Pharaoh grew furious.

"How can you believe in his God before I gave you my permission?" he asked them angrily.

The magicians replied, "Do what you wish but we fear the punishment of Allah much more than you."

The Pharaoh got angry when he heard this. He now realized that he had a problem, as the Prophet kept asking him to free the Israelites. He built his kingdom on the fear of Israelites and everyone believed him to be a god. He was now worried that his kingdom was about to be unraveled.

ALLAH'S PUNISHMENT TO EGYPTIANS

After the contest, the Pharaoh felt threatened from Musa^{alaihi-salam} but he became more arrogant. He summoned all the ministers and leaders for a serious meeting.

"Am I a liar, O Haman?" He opened the session with this question.

Haman stood up and asked, "Who dared to accuse you of lying?"

"Didn't Musa say that there is a Lord in Heaven?"

"Musa is lying." said Haman.

The pharaoh then ordered to kill and torture all those who followed the Prophet. The soldiers then started torturing Israelites. They slayed the men, and not even the babies were spared. They imprisoned anyone who dared to oppose them. The Prophet stood watching their horrific acts helplessly. He asked the people to be patient and have faith in Allah^{subhanahu wa ta'ala}.

Allah commanded Musa^{alaihi-salam} to warn the Pharaoh that he and the Egyptians would suffer a severe punishment if the children of Israel were not set free. The Prophet went to meet the Pharaoh again. He then made another demand to release the Israelites, but the Pharaoh refused. It was then that God afflicted Egypt with a severe drought. Even the lush green and fertile valleys of the Nile began to wither and die. The crops failed, and the animals died. Even as the Egyptians suffered because of the famine, the Pharaoh refused to obey and he remained arrogant. Then God sent a huge flood to devastate the land of Egypt. It drowned the villagers, the crops were destroyed, and many Egyptians were killed. Then the people including the chief ministers appealed to the Musa^{alaihi-salam}.

"Musa!" they cried. "Please help us! We shall believe in you and your God if you remove this punishment from us. We shall let the children of Israel go with you."

The Prophet then prayed to God and the land return to normal. It became fertile, and the crops grew again. But the children of Israel were still enslaved. They were not allowed to leave as promised. The Prophet asked them to fulfill their promise, but they paid no heed to his request. They ignored him and walked away.

He prayed to God again, and this time Allah send plagues of locusts to Egypt. The locusts attacked the crops and swallowed everything in their path. The people rushed to the Prophet begging for his help. The Ministers promised to let go off the Israelites if he would send the locust away. The Prophet prayed to God again, and the locust departed. But even now, they didn't let the Israelites leave as they promised. After that, God sent the plague of lice, spreading disease amongst the Egyptians. It was followed by a plague of frogs that harassed and terrified the people.

Every time God sent his punishment, the people rushed to the Prophet begging to save them. They promised to free the Israelites every time, but when God withdrew the punishments, they refused to let go off them. Then the last sign, "the sign of blood" was revealed. The water of the River Nile turned into the blood. The water appeared normal when the Israelites drank from the river. However, if any Egyptian filled his cup with water, the water turned into blood. They hurried to the Prophet as usual, and as soon as everything returns to normal, they turned their backs on Allah[subhanahu wa ta'ala].

The Egyptians refuse to believe in Allah despite the miracles that Musa[alaihi-salam] performed. Pharaoh's people would appeal to Musa[alaihi-salam] promising to release Israelites but time and again, they broke their promises.

THE EXODUS & THE PHARAOH'S DEMISE

Finally, God withdrew his mercy and gave order For Musa[alaihi-salam] to lead his people out of Egypt. The people carried their jewels and other belongings with them. This Mass Migration was later known as 'The Exodus'.

In the darkness of the night, the Prophet led his people towards the Red Sea. By now, Pharaoh realized that the Israelites had left the city. He got furious, and he assembled an army to follow and capture the Israelites.

By early morning, the Israelites had reached the Red Sea. When the Prophet Musa[alaihi-salam] looked back, he could see the Army getting closer and closer. He realized that they would soon get trapped. In front of them was the Red Sea, and to their back was Pharaoh's army.

Fear and Panic began to spread through the people. Musa[alaihi-salam] walked towards the edge of the Red Sea and looked out at the horizon. It was then that Yusha[alaihi-salam] turned to the Prophet Musa[alaihi-salam] and asked, "In front of us is this impassable barrier - the sea. And our enemy is approaching from behind. Surely, death cannot be avoided."

But the Prophet Musa[alaihi-salam] did not panic. He stood silently and waited for Allah[subhanahu wa ta'ala] to keep his promise - to free the children of Israel. At that moment, Allah commanded Musa[alaihi-salam] to strike the sea with his staff. Musa[alaihi-salam] did as he was commanded.

A fierce wind blew. The sea began to swirl and spin. And suddenly, the sea parted revealing a path for the people to walk. It was a miracle. Musa[alaihi-

^{salam} then led his people across the sea. As they walked, the wave stood like a mountain on each side. The prophet ensured that everyone crossed the sea safely. When he looked back, he could see the Pharaoh and his men approaching.

"Except for those who are patient and do righteous deeds; those will have forgiveness and great reward." [Hud 11:11]

The Pharaoh and his army had seen this miracle as well. But the Pharaoh was a pretender. He wanted to take credit for this miracle, so he shouted to his men, "Look! the sea has opened at my command, so that we may arrest them."

They rushed across the parted waters following the Israelites. But when they reached midway, water came crashing on them.

Pharaoh realized that he was going to die. He shouted out of fear, "I believe that there is no God other than Allah and I surrender to you."

But it was too late. The curtain fell on the Pharaoh's tyranny, and the waves carried his body to the shore. When the Egyptians saw his dead body, they realized that the man they had worshipped could not even keep away his own death. They now knew that he was never a god.

THE DEFIANCE OF ISRAELITES

God had favored the children of Israel and he led them safely out of Egypt. After a few days of walking in the desert, they got thirsty. God then commanded Musa^{alaihi-salam} to strike a rock with his staff. A miracle happened and there came twelve different springs of water from the rock. Each spring was meant for twelve different tribes. God did this so that there won't be any dispute while sharing the water. God also sent clouds to protect them from the scorching sun. And when they were hungry, he sent a special delicious food called Manna. But despite God's generosity, many people kept complaining to the Prophet.

Musa^{alaihi-salam} scolded the people and reminded them that they had just left the life of slavery. He asked them to be happy instead, and thank God for his generosity.

The children of Israelites were broken people, unable to stay away from sin and corruption. They were tired of Manna, and tired of the traveling. They wondered if there really was a place called 'Caanan' after all. The people kept traveling through the desert for days and days. They were walking with no destination, day and night, morning and evening. Eventually, they entered 'the Sinai'.

Musa^{alaihi-salam} realized that this was the place where he had spoken to God before his journey to Egypt. He decided to climb the mountain, so he called his brother Haroon^{alaihi-salam} and asked him to take charge of the people while he was gone. But before climbing the mountain, God ordered the

Prophet to fast for thirty days. On the thirtieth day, God then asked the Prophet to fast for ten more days. After the fast was completed, Musa^{alaihi-salam} was ready to speak to the Lord once again. He then started climbing the mountain. The Climb was long and difficult.

Once he reached the top, God gave him two tablets, in which the special laws to govern the Israelites were written. Musa^{alaihi-salam} had gone for forty days and the people grew restless. They were like children, complaining and acting impulsively. Among them, there was a man named 'Samiri', who was more inclined towards evil.

He suggested that they needed another guide, and he told them that the Prophet Musa^{alaihi-salam} had deserted them.

"In order to find true guidance, you need a true God!" he shouted this to the Israelites. "I shall provide you one." he started collecting all their jewelry at first. Then he dug a hole in the ground, in which he placed a lot, and put all the jewelry inside. Then, he lit a fire.

Samiri then made a golden calf out of the molten metal. It was as if they had succeeded in making a god.

Haroon^{alaihi-salam}, the brother of the Prophet Musa^{alaihi-salam} was afraid to stand up to the people at first. But when he saw the idol, he spoke up,

"You are committing a grave sin!" he shouted at them. He warned them of the consequences of their actions.

"We shall stop worshipping this god only when Musa^{alaihi-salam} returns." they replied.

Those who remained true to their belief separated themselves from the idol worshippers. They stood along with Haroon^{alaihi-salam}. When Musa^{alaihi-salam} returned, he saw his people dancing around the idol. His heart was filled with shame and anger now. He threw the tablets to the ground in his anger. He then tugged Haroon's beard and his hair crying, "What held you back when you saw them doing this? Why did you not fight them?"

"O son of my mother, let go of my beard. They were about to kill me." Musa^{alaihi-salam} understood Haroon's helplessness, and he began to handle the situation calmly and wisely. He called Samiri and said, "Get away from here. You shall live for the rest of your life alone." Musa^{alaihi-salam} sent him to exile forever. He knew that Allah would punish them for worshiping the idol. So, he chose seventy seniors from each tribe and ordered them.

"Rush towards Allah^{subhanahu wa ta'ala} and repent for what you have done." He then started climbing Mount Sinai with those seventy elders. Once they reached the top, the Prophet asked the elders to wait for him, and he walked ahead. There he started communicating with Allah^{subhanahu wa ta'ala}.

The elders could hear Musa^{alaihi-salam} speaking with God, but they could not see him. The Prophet returned after some time and the elders told him,

"O Musa! We shall never believe in you until we see Allah ourselves."

Their stubborn demand was rewarded with punishing thunderbolts and an earthquake, that killed all of them instantly. Musa^{alaihi-salam} was very sad now. He wondered what he would say to the children of Israelites. Those seventy men were the best of the people. So, he turned to God and prayed for forgiveness. Allah heard his prayers, and he raised the dead people back to life.

The children of Israel wandered in the desert for many years. Musa^{alaihi-salam} suffered greatly because of the ignorance of his people. He suffered everything for the sake of his people. Allah never let them reach the promised land because of the sins committed by the Israelites.

THE DEATH OF THE PROPHET MUSA^{ALAIHI-SALAM}

After a few years, Prophet Haroon^{alaihi-salam} died, while they were wandering in the desert. When the time of death for Prophet Musa^{alaihi-salam} arrived, the angel of death was sent to him. When the angel came to the Prophet, he slapped him on the eye. The angel returned to Lord and said, "You had sent me to a slave who didn't want to die."

Then Allah said, "Return to him now. When you meet him, ask him to put his hand on the back of an Ox. Tell him that for every hair that comes under his arm, he will be granted one year of life."

The angel returned to the Prophet and gave him Allah's message.

"What will happen after that?" Musa^{alaihi-salam} asked.

"Death." said the Angel.

"Then let it come now." replied the Prophet.

The Prophet then requested Allah^{subhanahu wa ta'ala} to let him die close to the Holy Land, so that he could at least see it from a distance. Allah granted his request, and he died shortly after.

Prophet Musa^{alaihi-salam}, the one to whom Allah^{subhanahu wa ta'ala} spoke directly, met his death with a contented soul and a faithful heart.

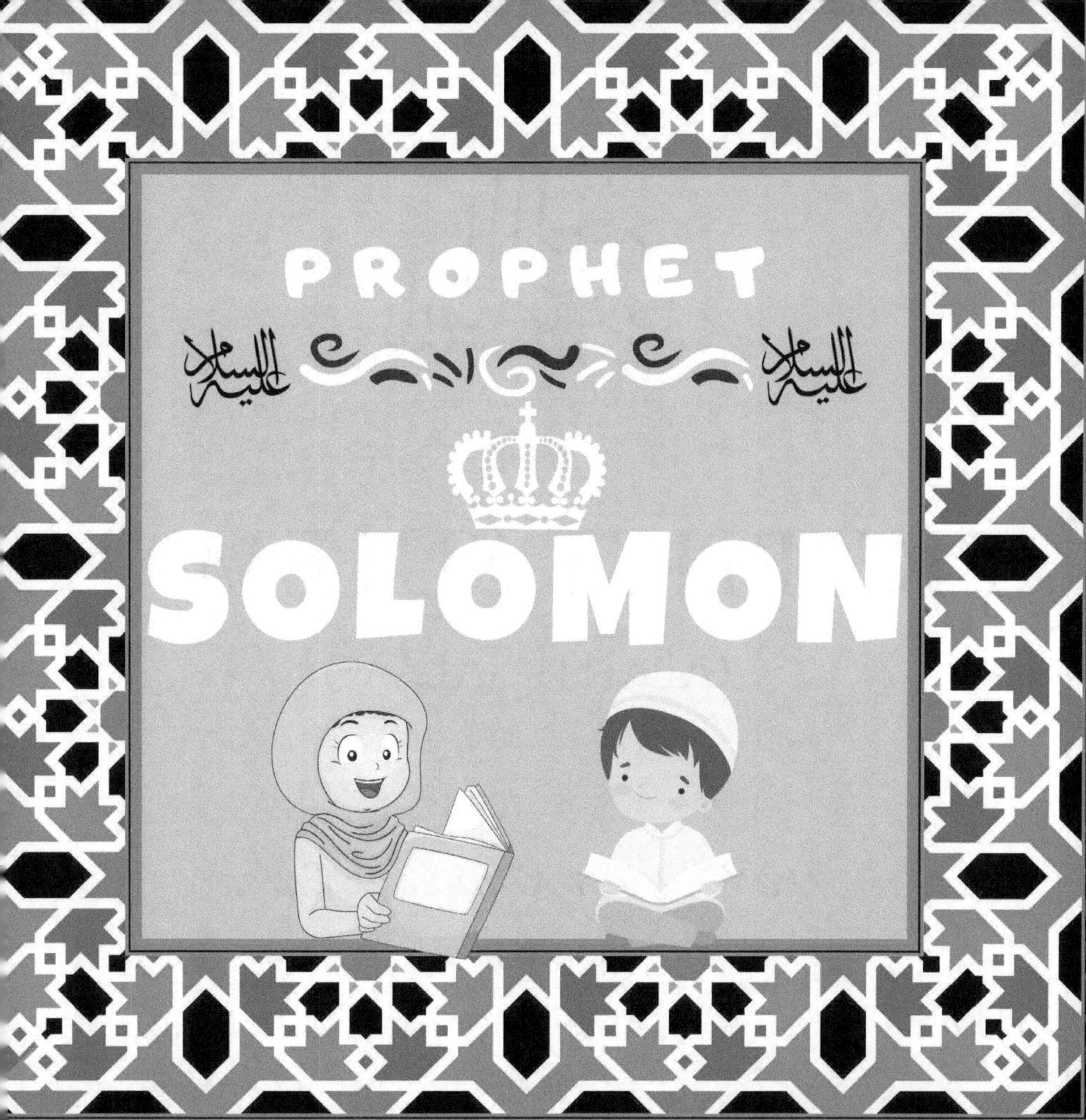

PROPHET SULEMAN

(ALAIHI SALAM)

The Greatest King Ever Ruled

Prophet Sulaiman (Solomon)^{alaihi salam} inherited Prophet Dawud's (David)^{alaihi salam} prophethood and dominion. This was not a material inheritance, as Prophets do not leave their property. It is given away to the poor and needy, not to their relatives.

Prophet Muhammad^{sallallaho alaihi wasallam} said,

"The Prophets' property will not be inherited, and whatever we leave is to be used for charity." (Sahih Al-Bukhari).

Prophet Sulaiman^{alaihi salam} was very intelligent since his childhood. One day, two people came with their case in front of Prophet Dawud^{alaihi salam} in the presence of Sulaiman^{alaihi salam}. One of them was a farmer, and the other was a poor shepherd. The farmer complained that the sheep of the poor shepherd grazed over his farm and caused significant damage. He requested compensation from the shepherd. Dawud^{alaihi salam} ordered the shepherd to give all of his sheep to the farmer as the compensation.

Sulaiman^{alaihi salam}, with due respect towards his father's judgment, took permission and humbly suggested another option. He suggested that the poor shepherd should take the farm and cultivate it and the farmer should keep the sheep and use their milk and wool. When the farm is restored to its original condition, the farmer should take back the farm and the sheep must be returned to the shepherd again. Dawud^{alaihi salam} was amazed by the solution and appreciated it and didn't hesitate to accept a suggestion from the child.

Prophet Dawud^{alaihi salam} was a wise king, and when he passed away, Prophet Sulaiman^{alaihi salam} became king. He pleaded Allah^{subhanahu wa ta'ala} for a kingdom so big and powerful, such as none after him would have, and Allah granted his wish. Besides wisdom, Allah had blessed Sulaiman^{alaihi salam} with many miracles. He could control the winds, and he could easily travel interminable distances within a brief period with the help of wind, and understand and talk to birds and animals. The Jinns, which are unseen creation from the eyes of humans now, were also under the command of Sulaiman^{alaihi salam}. He was the only person to whom Allah had granted the power to control Jinns. He could command them and utilize them for his service. He could even make them suffer for disobedience.

Allah^{subhanahu wa ta'ala} directed him to teach both men and jinns, to mine the earth and extract its minerals to make tools and weapons. He also favored him with a mine of copper, which was a rare metal in those days.

During that time, horses were the common mode of transportation. They were very essential for defense, to carry soldiers and cart provisions, and weapons of war. The animals were well cared for and well trained. One day, Sulaiman^{alaihi salam} was reviewing a parade of his stable. The fitness, beauty, and posture of the horses fascinated him so much that he kept on stroking and admiring them. This occupied his mind for some time which somehow affected his worship of Allah^{subhanahu wa ta'ala}. This made him realize that worldly things might affect the remembrance of Allah^{subhanahu wa ta'ala} and he repented towards Lord after that.

Once, Sulaiman^{alaihi salam} gathered his army, which had different battalions of men, jinns, birds, and animals. He marched them to the country of Askalon. While they were passing through a valley, an ant saw the approaching army and cried out to warn the other ants,

"Run to your homes! Otherwise, Sulaiman^{alaihi salam} and his army, unaware, might crush you!"

Sulaiman^{alaihi salam}, hearing the cry of the ant, smiled. He was glad that the ant knew him to be a Prophet who would not intentionally harm Allah's creation. He thanked Allah for saving the ants' lives.

THE ABSENSE OF HOOPOE (HUD-HUD)

In Jerusalem, on a huge rock, Sulaiman^{alaihi salam} built a beautiful temple to draw the people to worship Allah^{subhanahu wa ta'ala}. Today this building is known as "The Dome of the Rock." From there, a sizeable group of followers joined Sulaiman^{alaihi salam} on the pilgrimage to the Holy Mosque in Makkah. After they had completed their Hajj, they traveled to Yemen and arrived in the city of San'a. Their clever method of channeling water all over their cities impressed Sulaiman^{alaihi salam}. He was keen to build similar water systems in his own country but did not have enough springs.

He set out to find the hoopoe bird, which could detect water under the ground. One day, Sulaiman^{alaihi salam} had gathered his army comprising humans, animals, birds, jinns and of course wind. The sharp eyes of Sulaiman^{alaihi salam} noticed the absence of one hoopoe bird (hud-hud) in the huge gathering. He decided to severely punish or imposing death penalty to the bird as a non-disciplinary action, but he gave the bird a chance to explain the reason behind its absence. He sent signals all over the kingdom to call on him, but it was nowhere to be found.

The hoopoe eventually came to Sulaiman^{alaihi salam}, and explained the reason for its delay.

"I have discovered something of which you are not aware of. I have come from Sheba (Sab'a) with important news." Sulaiman^{alaihi salam} became curious, and his anger subsided.

The bird continued: "Beyond the knowledge of Sulaiman^{alaihi salam}, there is a kingdom named Sheba, which was being ruled by a Queen named 'Bilqis', who owned lots of things including a splendid Throne. But despite all this wealth, Satan has entered her heart and the hearts of her people. She rules their minds completely. It shocked me to learn that they worship the sun instead of Allah, the Almighty."

To check the hoopoe's information, Sulaiman^{alaihi salam} sent a letter to the Queen with the bird and waited for the response. He instructed the bird to remain hidden and to watch everything.

سُلَيْمَان
(Sulaymān)

THE QUEEN OF SHEBA

The hoopoe dropped the letter in front of the Queen and flew away to hide. She opened and read it:

"Verily! It is from Sulaiman, and verily!" It reads: 'In the Name of Allah, the Most Beneficent, and Most Merciful; be you not exalted against me, but come to me as Muslims (true believers who submit with full submission).'" (Ch 27:30-31 Quran).

The Queen of Sheba (Bilqis) was really intelligent. After receiving the letter, she discussed the matter with her chiefs and sought their counsels. The chiefs suggested that they are powerful enough to fight back in response. They reacted as to a challenge, for they felt that someone was challenging them, hinting at war and defeat, and asking them to submit to his conditions. They told her that they could only offer advice, but it was her right to command action. She sensed that they wanted to meet Sulaiman's invasion threat with a battle. But she told them:

"Peace and friendship are better and wiser; war only brings humiliation, enslaves people and destroys the good things. I have decided to send gifts to Sulaiman, selected from our most precious treasure. The courtiers who will deliver the gifts will also have an opportunity to learn about Sulaiman and his military might."

This was a sign of her great diplomatic approach to handling situations with intelligence and not with arrogance of strength & power.

Sulaiman^{alaihi salam} reconnaissance team brought him the news of the arrival of Bilqis' messengers with a gift. He immediately realized that the Queen had sent her men on a probing mission. Thus, he gave orders to rally the army. The envoys of Bilqis, entering amidst the well-equipped army, realized that their wealth was nothing compared to that of the Kingdom of Prophet Sulaiman^{alaihi salam}. His palace floors were made of sandalwood and inlaid with gold.

They noticed Sulaiman^{alaihi salam} surveying his army, and they were surprised at the number and variety of soldiers, which included lions, tigers, and birds too. The messengers stood in amazement, realizing that they were in front of an irresistible army.

The envoys marveled at the splendor surrounding them. They eagerly presented their Queen's precious gifts and told Sulaiman^{alaihi salam} that the Queen wished that he would accept them as an act of friendship.

He told them:

"Allah^{subhanahu wa ta'ala} has given me plenty of wealth, a large kingdom, and Prophethood. I am, therefore, beyond bribery. My only aim is to spread the belief in Tawheed, the Oneness of Allah."

Sulaiman^{alaihi salam} did not even ask to open the covers of the containers which contained precious gifts! His reaction shocked them.

He directed them to take back the gifts to the Queen, and tell her that if she did not stop worshipping the Sun, he would uproot her kingdom and drive its people out of the land.

سُلَيْمَان
(Sulaymān)

The Queen's envoys returned with the gifts and delivered the message. They also told her of the wonderful things they had seen. Instead of taking offense, she decided to visit Prophet Sulaiman^{alaihi salam}. Accompanied by her royal officials and servants, she left Sheba, sending a messenger ahead to inform Sulaiman^{alaihi salam} that she was on her way to meet him.

Sulaiman^{alaihi salam} asked the jinns in his employ whether anyone among them could bring her throne to his palace before she arrives.

One of them said; "I will bring it to you before this sitting is over."

Sulaiman^{alaihi salam} did not react to this offer; it appeared that he was waiting for a faster means. The jinns competed with each other to please him.

One of them named 'Ifrit', said: "I will fetch it for you in the twinkling of an eye!"

No sooner had this one - who had the knowledge of the Book - finished his phrase than the throne stood before Sulaiman^{alaihi salam}. The mission had, indeed, been completed in the blinking of an eye. Prophet Sulaiman^{alaihi salam} seat was in Palestine, and the throne of Bilqis had been in Yemen, two thousand miles away. This was a great miracle performed by one of those believers sitting with Sulaiman^{alaihi salam}. After that, Sulaiman^{alaihi salam} instructed the Jinns to make slight alterations to the throne to check whether Bilqis would be able to identify it.

When Bilqis arrived at Sulaiman^{alaihi salam} palace, she was welcomed with pomp and ceremony. Then, pointing to the altered throne, Sulaiman^{alaihi salam} asked her whether her throne looked like that one. She looked at it again and again. In her mind, she was convinced that her throne could not possibly be the one she was looking at, as hers was in her palace. She detected a striking similarity and replied: "It is as if it were the very one and resembles mine in every respect." Sulaiman^{alaihi salam} judged that she was intelligent and diplomatic.

He then invited her into the majestic hall, the floor of which was laid in glass and shimmering. Some narration reports that the passages of glass had water-streams beneath it containing fish and other underwater creatures (just like an aquarium). She thought it was water, so she lifted her dress slightly above her heels so that they do not get wet. Sulaiman^{alaihi salam} assured her that the floor was built of glass. Some narrations say that he told it so that Bilqis does not uncover her legs in front of Sulaiman^{alaihi salam}, thus protecting her modesty.

It amazed her. She had never seen such things before. Bilqis realized that she was in the company of a very knowledgeable person who was not only a ruler of a great kingdom but a messenger of Allah^{subhanahu wa ta'ala}, as well. She repented, gave up sun worship, accepted the faith of Allah, and asked her people to do the same. Bilqis saw her people's creed fall apart before Sulaiman^{alaihi salam}. She realized that the sun which her people worshipped was nothing but one of Allah's creations.

THE DEATH OF PROPHET
SULAIMAN^{ALAIHI SALAM}

Sulaiman^{alaihi salam} public work was largely carried out by the jinns. He used to command the Jinns to build publicly visible structures like arches, images, basins, and enormous cooking pots. Also, this was a punishment for their sins of making people believe that they were all-powerful, knew the unseen, and could foresee the future. As a Prophet, it was Sulaiman^{alaihi salam} duty to remove such false beliefs from his followers, so they should not worship any of Allah's creations.

Prophet Sulaiman^{alaihi salam} lived amidst glory, and all creatures were subjected to him. Then Allah, the Exalted, ordained for him to die. His life and death were full of wonders and miracles; thus, his death harmonized with his life and glory. His death, like his life, was unique.

Once, he was sitting holding his staff, overseeing the jinns at work in a mine. His soul was taken away while sitting in this position. For a long time, no one was aware of his death, for he was seen sitting erect. The Jinns kept on doing their work for a long time, thinking that Sulaiman^{alaihi salam} was watching over them, sitting erect over his staff. This indicates that the future and unseen in not known by any jinn or human but by Allah alone and whoever Allah wishes to bestow the knowledge.

Many days later, a hungry ant began nibbling Sulaiman^{alaihi salam} staff. It continued to do so, eating the lower part of the staff, until it fell out of

Prophet's hand, and as Sulaiman^{alaihi salam} was leaning on the staff, his great body came down to the ground. People hurried to him, realizing that he had died a long time ago and that the jinns did not perceive the unseen, for had the jinns known the unseen, they would not have kept working, thinking that Sulaiman^{alaihi salam} was alive.

PROPHET ISA
(ALAIHI SALAM)

The Healer & Resurrector

عِيسَى
(' Īsā)

The importance of the Prophet Isa^{alaihi-salam} is apparent from the status assigned to him. He was the last messenger and prophet before Prophet Muhammad^{Salallahu alaihi wasalam}. He was also the last messenger of Bani-Israel. Allah had bestowed a special favor on the family of Prophet Isa^{alaihi-salam} by mentioning his name 25 times. His mother's name is mentioned 31 times as well.

PIOUS MARYAM^{ALAIHI-SALAM} AND THE BIRTH OF PROPHET ISA^{ALAIHI-SALAM}

Maryam^{alaihi-salam} was the daughter of the Prophet Imran^{alaihi-salam}. Prophet Zakaria^{alaihi-salam} took care of this little girl and built a separate room for her in the temple. As Maryam^{alaihi-salam} grew up, she spent her time in devotion to Allah^{subhanahu wa ta'ala}. The Prophet Zakaria^{alaihi-salam} visited her daily to see her needs, and it continued for many years. He taught and guided her. Maryam^{alaihi-salam} grew to be a devotee of Allah, glorifying him day and night.

One day Maryam^{alaihi-salam} was praying in her room as usual. It was then that an Angel appeared before her in the form of a man.

Maryam^{alaihi-salam} was terrified, thinking that this man was here to harm her.

She shouted, "I Seek refuge with Allah from you if you do fear Allah."

عِيسَى
('Īsā)

Then the angel said, "I am only a messenger of your lord to you. I was sent to give you a pious child who is pure from sins."

She had calm down by now. She asked the angel, "How can I have a son when no man has touched me?"

"That is very easy for Allah. Allah will make him a sign for the people and an indication of the power of Allah." The Angel's visit made her very tensed, which increases as days passed by.

After a few months, she could not bear the mental strain any longer. Burdened with a heavy womb, she left the city not knowing where to go. Maryam^{alaihi-salam} had not gone far when she was suddenly overtaken by the pains of childbirth. She sat down against the dry palm tree and it was here that she gave birth to a son.

When Maryam^{alaihi-salam} looked at her newborn baby, she was hurt.

"How could she bring him into this world without a father!" she exclaimed. "I wish I had died before this happened and just vanished."

Suddenly, she heard the voice of an Angel, "Grieve not," the voice said, " Allah^{subhanahu wa ta'ala} has placed a small river under you. And shake the trunk of this tree from which ripe dates will fall. Eat, and drink, and regain the strength you have lost. What you see is the power of Allah^{subhanahu wa ta'ala}."

Maryam^{alaihi-salam} drank water from the river and ate the ripe dates. For a while, Allah's miracle comforted her. After some time, she stood up and decided to return to the city. However, her fears also returned.

"What was she going to tell the people?" she thought.

It was then that another miracle happened. Her baby born just a few hours ago started to speak.

The baby said, "If you meet any person, just tell them that you have vowed to fast for Allah today and that you will not speak to anyone." With this miracle, Maryam^{alaihi-salam} felt at ease and walked towards the city.

A MIRACLE BY A CHILD

As she expected, her arrival in the city with a newborn baby in her arms, aroused the curiosity of the people.

"This is a terrible sin you have committed!" They scolded her, but she kept her calm. She put her fingers on her lips gesturing that she can't talk and pointed to her child.

The people were angry. "How can we speak to a newborn baby!"

But it surprised the people when the child began to speak. The child spoke slowly and clearly.

"I am Allah's servant. Allah^{subhanahu wa ta'ala} has given me the book and made me a prophet. Allah has made me dutiful towards her, who gave birth to me. Peace unto me the day I was born, the day I die, And the day I shall be raised alive." The people just stood there in wonder, watching the child speak.

They realized that the child was unique, and that it was Allah's will. Of course, some regarded the baby's speech as a strange trick.

But at least Maryam^{alaihi-salam} could now stay in the city without being harassed.

It is said that Yusuf, the carpenter was greatly surprised when he heard about this incident.

"Can a tree grow without a seed?" he asked her.

"Yes," she replied. "The one which Allah^{subhanahu wa ta'ala} created for the first time, grew without a seed."

Then he asked her again, "Is it possible to bear a child without a male partner?"

"Yes," Maryam^{alaihi-salam} replied. " Allah^{subhanahu wa ta'ala} created Adam^{alaihi-salam} without a male or a female."

THE YOUTH OF PROPHET ISA^{ALAIHI-SALAM}

As Prophet Isa^{alaihi-salam} grew up, his prophecy skills began to increase too. He could tell his friends what they would eat for supper, and what they had hidden and where.

When he was 12 years old, he accompanied his mother to Jerusalem. When they arrived at the temple, he wandered into the temple leaving his mother. The young prophet wandered into a room where people were listening to the lectures of priests. Even though the audience was full of adults, the prophet was not afraid to sit with them.

After listening to them for some time, he stood up and started asking questions. The questions he asked, disturbed the learned priests for they could not answer them.

The priests tried to silence him, but the prophet ignored them. He continued to ask questions and expressed his opinion. Prophet Isa^{alaihi-salam} got so involved in this exchange that he completely forgot about his mother.

Meanwhile, Maryam^{alaihi-salam} went home thinking that her son might have gone back with their relatives or friends. But as soon as she reached home, she realized that her son was not there. So, she ran to the city to find him. She searched for many hours and finally found her son sitting among the learned and debating with them. Maryam^{alaihi-salam} got very angry with him as she was worried so much. But the young prophet calmed her saying that he lost track of time while he was debating with the priests.

Prophet Isa^{alaihi-salam} studied the Torah earnestly. He was a pious worshipper of Allah^{subhanahu wa ta'ala} and followed the rules of Torah strictly. Once on the day of the Sabbath, Prophet Isa^{alaihi-salam} was on his way to the temple as Prophet Musa^{alaihi-salam} had commanded that one should dedicate Saturday for worshipping Allah. However, the wisdom behind the Sabbath had long gone by now. The priests now made a hundred things unlawful as they wished. Imagine this, it was considered against the law, if a doctor was called to save a dying patient. It was a sin to eat, drink or even plait the hairs.

But the prophet didn't care for their laws. He plucked the fruit to feed a hungry child. When the priest saw this, they frowned in anger. He made a fire for the old woman to keep themselves warm from freezing and this was considered being a violation of the Sabbath law. When the prophet finally arrived at the temple, he was surprised to find over 20,000 priests inside the temple. All of them earned a living from the temple alone.

Prophet Isa^{alaihi-salam} was surprised that there was more priest than visitors itself. Yet the temple was full of sheep and doves which was sold to the people to be offered as sacrifices. Every step inside the temple cost the visitor money. The prophet was sad to find the priests worshipped nothing but money. The priests were acting as if it was a marketplace.

The prophet saw the poor people who could not afford the price of a dove or sheep, were driven away like flies. The prophet was sad wondering why the priests burned such a huge number of offerings inside the temple while thousands of poor people were hungry outside.

THE BEGINNING OF THE REVELATIONS & THE OPPOSITION OF THE PRIESTS

It was on this night that the two noble prophets, Prophet Yahyah[alaihi-salam] and Prophet Zakaria[alaihi-salam] got killed by the Ruling Authority. That night the Revelation descended upon Prophet Isa[alaihi-salam]. Allah[subhanahu wa ta'ala] commanded the prophet to begin his call to the people of Israel. The simple life that the prophet had been living until now was over. The page of worship and the struggle was opened in the life of Isa[alaihi-salam].

Like an opposing force, Isa[alaihi-salam] denounced the current practices and reinforced the law of Prophet Musa[alaihi-salam]. The prophet asked his people to lead a simple life, by noble words and deeds. The prophet tried to make the priests understand that the Ten Commandments have more value than they imagined. For instance, he told them that the fifth commandment doesn't only prohibit physical killing but all forms of killing; physical, psychological or spiritual. His teachings annoyed the priests. For every word of the Prophet, was a threat to their position. Their misdeeds were getting exposed.

The priests started to plot against the prophet. One day, they arrested a woman accused of adultery. They then called Isa[alaihi-salam] to ask his opinion. They were actually planning to embarrass the prophet in front of the people. According to Mosaic law, a person involved in adultery had to be stoned to death. The priests knew that the prophet would oppose killing this woman and thereby, the prophet would end up speaking against the Mosaic law.

They brought the adulteress in front of Isa^{alaihi-salam} and asked him, "Doesn't the law stipulates the stoning of the adulteress?"

"Yes," the Prophet replied. He then looked at the priests and the people standing around. He knew that they were more sinful than this woman who was trying to earn a bread. He realized that if he speaks against them, then he would be held in contempt of Mosaic law. He now understood their plan. The prophet then smiled and spoke loudly to the people standing around, "Whoever among you is sinless can stone her."

The priests were surprised to hear this. The people standing around hesitated. No one present there dared to stone her, for they were all sinners.

There was no one eligible, for no mortal can judge sin. Only Allah^{subhanahu wa ta'ala}, the most merciful can judge. The prophet had made a new law on adultery that day. As the prophet left the temple, the woman followed him. The prophet realized that he was being followed. So, he stopped and asked her why she was following him. The woman remained silent and took out a bottle of perfume from her garment. She knelt before the prophet and washed his feet with the perfume and her own tears. She then dried his feet with her hair.

Her action touched Isa^{alaihi-salam}, and he asked her to stand up. The prophet then looked up and prayed, "O Lord! forgive her sins."

Prophet Isa^{alaihi-salam} continued to pray to Allah^{subhanahu wa ta'ala} for mercy on his people. He taught his people to show mercy on one another and to believe in Allah.

عيسى

(ʿĪsā)

Once he told his followers, "I sleep while I have nothing and I rise while I have nothing, and yet there is no one on earth who is wealthier than me."

NUMEROUS MIRACLES OF PROPHET
ISA^{ALAIHI-SALAM}

Like all other Prophets, Prophet Isa^{alaihi-salam} too performed many miracles. Allah^{subhanahu wa ta'ala} sent all the prophets with miracles as a proof to their prophethood. This way the people could witness, know about them, and believe in their prophethood. Many of the miracles that Prophet Isa^{alaihi-salam} performed were by curing illness. The people during this time were quite knowledgeable in the field of medicine. And when the prophet cured the sick who were declared untreatable, it sent out a sound message.

Prophet Isa^{alaihi-salam} once walked by a man who was blind, leprous and paralyzed. The Prophet heard him saying, "Praise be to Allah who has protected me from the trials, which he afflicts most men."

The Prophet stopped walking and asked him, "Tell me which trial do you remain to be afflicted with? You are blind, leprous and paralyzed."

But the beggar replied, "He protected me from a trial which is the greatest of all trials and that is disbelief."

The prophet was happy with this poor old man. He stepped forward and placed his hand on the poor man's shoulders. It was a miracle. As soon as the Prophet touched the man, his diseases cured, and he was able to stand up. Allah^{subhanahu wa ta'ala} even transformed him, that his face now shone with beauty. The old man sought permission from the Prophet to accompany him and he agreed. The old man became a companion of Prophet Isa^{alaihi-salam} and started worshipping with him.

Once, he put his hand on the face of a man who was born blind. He was cured and could see for the first time in his life.

One day, when the Prophet was walking to the town. He saw a procession taking place. The Prophet approached and asked them what was going on.

"This man is dead and we are taking him to the burial site." replied one of them.

The Prophet asked them to stop and prayed to Allah. It was a miracle. The dead man stood up, and he was alive. Allah brought this person back to life.

Prophet Isa^{alaihi-salam} had been following the Torah until he received the Revelation from God. God gave him a new book, "The Injil (Bible)". The Prophet then read this book which has been gifted to him. When the Prophet announced that he had received a new book from God, the people who still follow the Torah, did not like this.

عِيسَى
(ʿĪsā)

THE SPREAD OF FOOD FROM THE SKY

One day, Prophet Isa^{alaihi-salam} asked his supporters to fast for 30 days. His followers agreed, and they started fasting. Upon completion of thirty days fasting period, the followers went along with Prophet Isa^{alaihi-salam} to the desert. It was normal for thousands of people to follow the Prophet wherever he went. Many of the followers with Prophet were sick people, who hope to be cured by him. A group of people who were against the teachings of the Prophet, also followed him wherever he went. They followed him so that they could mock at the Prophet and belittle him at every opportunity they got.

After the thirty-day fasting period, the disbelievers asked the prophet, if they could have a spread of food from the sky. They asked for this to disprove that God had accepted their fast. There were thousands of people present there and the disbelievers knew that the Prophet could never deliver what they had asked for. They wanted to eat something special on the day they broke their fast. They also wanted the spread to be enough for all of them.

Prophet Isa^{alaihi-salam} agreed to their request and went to a silent spot, and prayed to Allah^{subhanahu wa ta'ala.} Allah accepted the prayers of Prophet and a miracle happened. A huge spread of food descended right from the sky. There was one cloud below the spread and one cloud above it, and it was surrounded by the angels. Slowly it came down to the ground, and as it descended, the Prophet remained immersed in his prayers.

The spread of food landed near the Prophet. There was a white cloth covering the spread. The Prophet took this off saying, "In the name of Allah, the best Sustainer!"

When the cloth covering the spread was taken off, the people gathered around and looked at in wonder. There were seven big fish, seven loaves of bread, vinegar, salt, honey, and many other fruits as well. The spread had a wonderful smell, as people had never smelled anything so wonderful before. The prophet then asked the disbelievers to eat from the spread.

"We will not eat from it until we see you eating from the spread." they replied.

"You are the ones who asked for it," the Prophet said. "Then you should eat the food first."

But the disbelievers still refused. The Prophet then asked the poor, the sick, the handicapped and the blind to eat from the spread. There were over 1,000 of them and all of them ate from the spread. All the sick people who ate from the spread, got cured. The same was the case with the handicapped, the blind and all others. It was a miracle. The disbelievers were now sad because they had refused to eat from the spread when they were invited first.

The news of the feast traveled fast and reached the city. Thousands of people traveled to witness this divine feast. The number of people who wanted to take part in the feast had now become so huge. The Prophet then ask them to take turns to have this feast. Days passed, as each person from the very first to the very last, ate until they were full. It is said that almost 7,000 people ate from the feast each day.

After forty days, Allah asked the Prophet to allow only the poor to eat from the feast, and not the rich. The Prophet warned the people to be honest and ask the rich to stay away from the feast. He also asked the poor not to take away the food to save for the next day.

However, people didn't listen. The rich people ate from the spread pretending to be poor and many poor people took the food with them disobeying the Prophet's orders. As a result, the spread of food was lifted back into the sky where it came from. The people talked about this miracle for many years, and it convinced them about Allah's miracles.

THE RISE OF PROPHET ISA^{ALAIHI-SALAM} TO THE HEAVENS

By the time Prophet Isa^{alaihi-salam} was thirty years old, the priests have become furious at him and they made plans to kill the Prophet. One night, the prophet was sitting along with his twelve companions in his house.

He said, "One among you is going to betray me."

It was true, and it was none other than Judas. Judas had gone to meet the head priests that day.

"What will you give me if I deliver Isa to you?" Judas asked the priest.

"We will give you thirty pieces of shekels." the head priest replied.

Judas was ashamed of himself. He left the room. Prophet Isa^{alaihi-salam} then asked any one of his companions was ready to take his place, as the soldiers were coming to arrest him.

"Who among you will be ready to take my place?" asked the Prophet. "You will be my companion in paradise."

A youthful man stood up and readily agreed. When the soldiers arrived to arrest the Prophet, they took the young man instead, and crucified him.

Before they crucified the young man, Prophet Isa^{alaihi-salam} was raised from a window in the house's corner. He is now alive in the second heaven. He shall descend before the Day of Judgement.

We, (as Muslims) believe that Prophet Isa^{alaihi-salam} will return to the earth as a human being. He will return just as he was taken up from the earth and will go after the anti-Christ (Dajjal) to slay him. He will then rule with justice and fairness in accordance with the teachings of Islam.

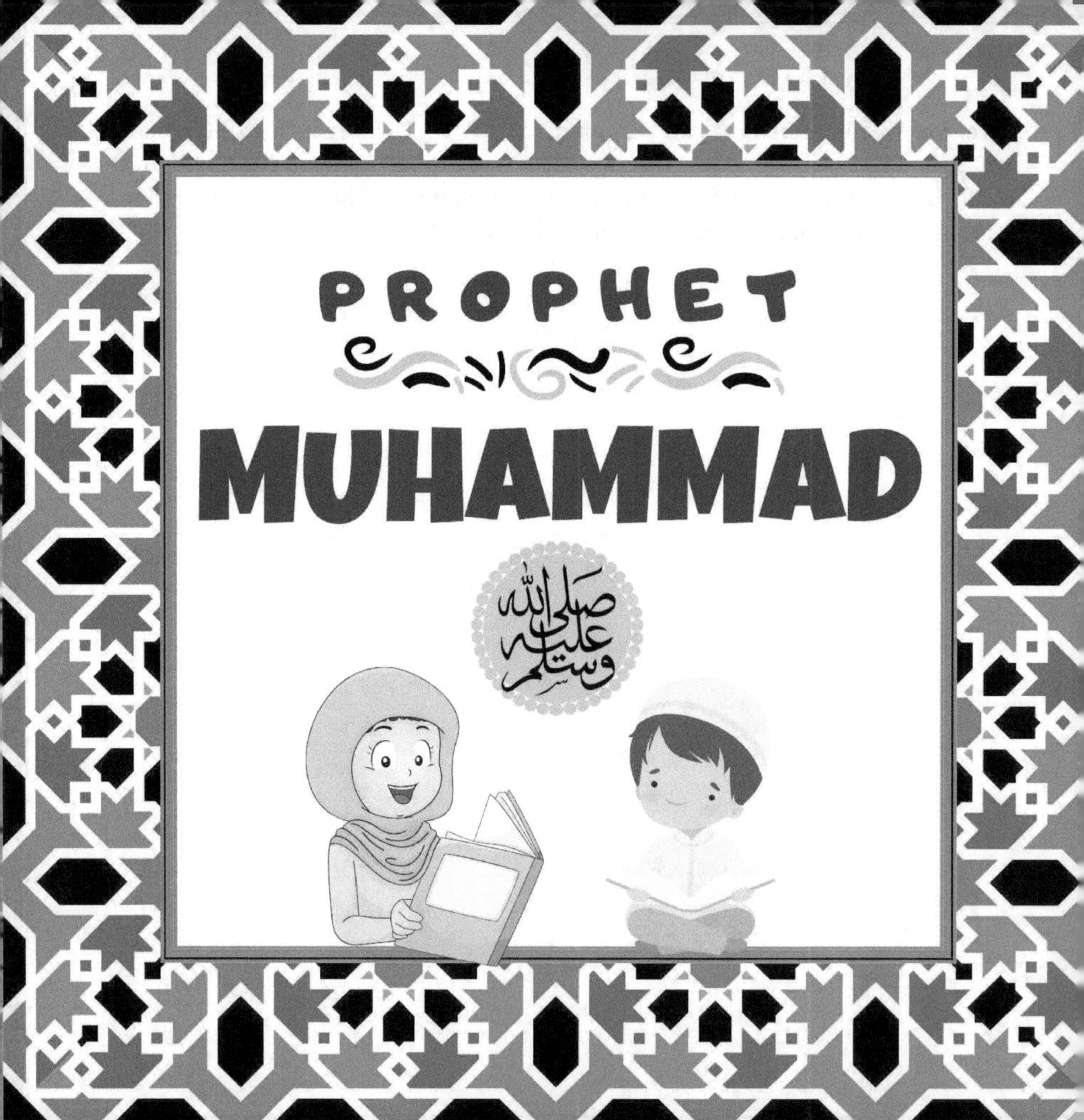

PROPHET
MUHAMMAD

(PEACE BE UPON HIM)

The Last Messenger & A Revolutionist for Humankind

Prophet Muhammad^{sallallaho alaihi wasallam} was born in Makkah, Arabia on 12th, Rabi-ul-Awwal. His mother, Amina^{radi Allaho anha}, was the daughter of Wahab Ibn Abu Manaf of the Zahrah family. His father Abdullah^{radi Allaho anho} was the son of Abdul Muttalib^{radi Allaho anho}. His ancestors can be traced to the noble house of Prophet Ismail^{alaihi salam}, the son of Prophet Ibrahim^{alaihi salam}.

The prophet's father died before he was born. His mother took care of him till the age of six. By the time he turned six, his mother also passed away. His grandfather Abdul Mutallib took tender care of the orphan child. But the old chief passed away in the next two years and before his death, he put the little one in charge of his uncle Abu Talib.

Prophet Muhammad^{sallallaho alaihi wasallam} grew up as an obedient boy. When he was twelve years old, he accompanied his uncle Abu Talib on his journey to Basra. They traveled for many months in the desert. When he introduced Prophet Muhammad^{sallallaho alaihi wasallam} to a monk, he was very impressed. He then said to Abu Talib, "Return with this boy and guard him against the hatred of Jews. A great career awaits your nephew."

Abu Talib didn't quite understand what the monk had meant. His nephew was just a normal child. He thanked and returned to Makkah. After this journey, nothing special happened in the life of this young prophet for a long time, but all authorities agree that he had great wisdom, manners, and morals, which was rare among the people of Makkah. Everyone liked him for

his good character and wisdom that he received the title of 'Ameen', which means the faithful, and 'Sadiq', which means the truthful.

Like every other child, he had to do the chores in his family. His uncle had lost most of his wealth and the prophet helped him by taking care of his flocks. Prophet Muhammad^{sallallaho alaihi wasallam} mostly led a solitary life. He was sad when he saw the sudden outbursts of bloody quarrels among the people of Makkah. The people didn't care about the law. His heart grieved when he saw the misery of other people, and such scenes were a daily occurrence in Makkah during that time.

MARRIAGE PROPOSAL BY

KHADIJA^{RADI ALLAHO ANHA}

When the prophet was twenty-five years old, he traveled once again to Syria, and it was here that he met the love of his life, Khadija^{radi Allaho anha}.

Khadija^{radi Allaho anha} was one of the most beautiful and noble woman around. She was from a very wealthy family, but she was a widow. Despite being a widow, many wealthy and prominent men in the society asked her hand in marriage, but she rejected them all as she had lost the desire to marry again. It was only until Prophet Muhammad^{salallahu alaihi wasallam}, entered her life. At that time, Khadija^{radi Allaho anha} was looking for someone honest who could conduct business for her. It was then that she got introduced to the prophet. She learned that even though he was an orphan and poor, he came from a noble family. This man was of impeccable moral character and widely known as the most honest man around.

Prophet Muhammad^{sallallaho alaihi wasallam} soon started working for her and set out for his first business trip along with her servant. After they came back, she asked the servant about the prophet's conduct. The servant amazed her by his report.

"This young man is the kindest I have ever seen." he said, "He never treated me harshly as many others do and when we were traveling in the desert under the scorching sun, there was always a cloud following us providing us the shade. Not only that, but this new employee also proved to be a talented

businessman. First, he sold the merchandise she gave to him. Then with the profit, he bought other merchandise and resold them again. Thus, making a double profit. Khadija fell deeply in love with the prophet even though he was 15 years younger. She resolved to marry him.

The next day, she sent his sister to this young man.

"Why are you not married yet?" she asked him.

"For lack of means." he answered.

"What if I were to offer you a wife of nobility and beauty? Will you be interested?" she asked.

"Who is it?" he replied.

When she mentioned her sister, the young man chuckled in amazement.

"How could I marry her? She has turned down the noblest men in the city. They were much wealthier and prominent than this poor shepherd."

But the sister replied, "Don't you worry, I will take care of it."

Not long after, the Prophet Muhammad$^{sallallaho\ alaihi\ wasallam}$ married Khadija$^{radi\ Allaho\ anha}$, it was the beginning of one of the most loving, happiest and sacred marriages in all human history. This marriage gave him the loving heart of a woman who consoled him and kept alive within him a flickering flame of hope when no man believed in him. The prophet lived a wealthy life for many years. After that, when the prophet reached the age of 35, he settled a grave dispute by his judgment, which threatened to plunge Arabia into a fresh series of war. It was the time for rebuilding the Ka'aba. Every tribe who had gathered there, wanted the honor of raising the

Blackstone-the most holy Relic. The leaders and men of each tribe fought among themselves to claim the honor. Then a senior citizen intervened and said to the people,

"You will listen to the first man who enters through that gate." The people agreed and waited patiently looking at the gate. The first man to enter the gate was none other than Prophet Muhammad^{sallallaho alaihi wasallam}.

The different tribes sought his advice, and after they finished, the Prophet ordered, "Place the stone on a cloth. Each tribe shall have the honor of lifting the stone by holding a part of the cloth." The people happily agreed to this idea. The stone was thus placed, and they completed the rebuilding of the house without further Interruption.

It was during this time that a man named Osman Ibn Huwairith arrived in Makkah. He tried to tempt the people of Makkah by using Byzantine Gold, and tried to turn the territory depended on the Roman government. But his attempts failed because the prophet intervened and warn the people of Makkah.

The Prophet always help the poor and needy as well. It is said that when his uncle Abu Talib fell into bad times, the prophet cleared all his debts using personal wealth. The Prophet also undertook the education of his uncle's son, Ali, and brought him up. A year later, he adopted 'Akil', another one of his uncle's son.

The Prophet Muhammad^{sallallaho alaihi wasallam} from his humble beginnings, had now become wealthy and quite respected. Khadija^{radi Allaho anha} gave birth to

three sons and four daughters. But none of the male children survived. They all died in childhood itself.

The Prophet loved Ali very much, and he found consolation in him. It was during this time that a group of Arab plunderers captured Zaid, a young boy from the arms of his mother. These plunderers then sold the boy as a slave in the market of Ukaz'. A relative of Khadija bought Zaid, and he gave him as a gift to her. Khadijah in turn, gave the boy to the Prophet as a gift. The Prophet became very attached to Zaid, to whom he referred as "Al-Habib" which means 'the Beloved'.

Zaid considered the Prophet to be his mentor and followed his ways. The boy had a spiritual mind and good morals of the Prophet. In the meantime, Zaid's parents were still grieving at the loss of their son. They prayed daily that their beloved son would be returned to them.

One day, the parents of Zaid visited Makkah to perform the pilgrimage. It was here that they spotted Zaid and with great relief, they rushed towards him. When his father came to know about this wonderful news, he loaded his bags with gold and approached Prophet Muhammad^{sallallaho alaihi wasallam}. The father thought he can buy his son back from his owner. Zaid father met and asked him to release his boy.

The Prophet asked him, "Who is this person whose release you are demanding?"

"Your slave, Zaid Ibn Haritha." replied the father.

"Shall I show you a way by which you can get your son back without paying the gold."

It surprised the Father. He asked, "What is this way you are talking about?"

"I will call him here in front of you. If he wishes to go with you then he is free to do so. You can take him gladly and I will take no payment from you, but..." The prophet continued, "If he prefers to stay with me, then I will not force him to go with you."

Zaid's father agreed, and they called the boy. The Prophet then explained to him the choices he had and asked him to decide.

"I will stay with you." the boy said at once.

His father was shocked to hear this.

Then he asked him, "Don't you want to stay with your parents? or do you prefer to stay as a slave?"

"Father…" said the boy, "I am deeply moved by the qualities of this man. And by the way, he treats me with love and affection. I can never leave him and live anywhere else." the Prophet's heart swelled when he heard this. He led Zaid to the Center of the town and claimed loudly, "This is my son. And we inherit each other."

As a result, Zaid Ibn Haritha was renamed Zaid bin Muhammed, as it was customary during those days. This cordial relationship lasted till his last breath.

THE RELEVATION FROM ALLAH

Prophet Muhammad^{sallallaho alaihi wasallam} was approaching the age of 40. He was very sad looking at the condition of his people. His country was torn into wars, and the people were in barbarism. They were addicted to superstitions and idol-worshipping. The people were always fighting with each other. The Prophet had a habit of secluding himself in a cave on Mount Hira, just a few miles from Makkah. He used to pray and meditate inside this cave, most of the time alone. Here he often spent the nights in deep thought and profound communion with the All-knowing Allah of the universe.

It was during one of these nights when no one was near him, that an angel appeared before him. The sight of the Angel amazed the Prophet. He couldn't believe his eyes. The angel then asked the Prophet to read. But how could the Prophet read when he had never gone to school?

"I'm not a reader." he said to the angel.

Then suddenly the angel took hold of him and squeezed him tightly. The angel said again, "Read."

"I'm not a reader." the Prophet cried again. The angel then squeezed the Prophet so hard that he thought that he would faint.

 The angel said, "Read! In the name of your lord and cherisher, who created man out of a clot of congealed blood. Read! And your lord is the most generous, who has taught writing by the pen, taught man which he knew not."

The Prophet repeated the words with a trembling heart. Perplexed by his experience, the prophet made his way home. As soon as he entered his house, he said to his wife, "Wrap me up! Wrap me up!"

He was trembling as he said this, and she wrapped him up in a towel until his fear was gone. He explained to his wife what had happened. When he finished, he asked her if she thought he had gone mad.

"Allah forbid!" she replied. "He will surely not let such a thing happen, for you speak the truth. You are faithful to trust. You aid your fellow men."

Then she went to her cousin, Warqa bin Naufil, who was old and blind, but he knew the scriptures quite well. He had translated them into Arabic. When she told him about what happened to her husband, he cried out,

"Holy! Holy! This is the holy spirit that came to Moses. He will be the Prophet for his people. Tell him this and ask him to be brave at heart."

The Prophet continued to receive revelations for the rest of his life. It was memorized and written down by his companions on sheepskins. The Prophet knew that the people had to hear the message from God. So, he started preaching to the people what God told him. For the first few years of his mission, the Prophet preached to his family and close friends. The first woman to convert was his wife Khadija^{radi Allaho anha}, and the first bondsman was his servant, Zaid^{radi Allaho anho}. His old friend Abu Bakr^{radi Allaho anho} was the first adult free male to convert.

Many years later, the Prophet Muhammad^{sallallaho alaihi wasallam} said this about him. "I have never called anyone to Islam who was not at first hesitant, except Abu Bakr^{radi Allaho anho}."

For three long years, the Prophet labored quietly to deliver the message of God. Idol worshipping was deeply rooted among the people and the Prophet tried to convince as much as he could. After three years of struggle, he was only able to secure 13 followers. Later, the prophet received the command to preach openly. Even his companions had now started questioning his sanity. By now his enemies had started plotting against him. He preached that everyone was equal in front of God, and this challenged the authority of local priests.

One day, they gathered together and decided to suppress the movement of the Prophet. They decided that each family should take upon themselves the task of stamping out the followers of Islam. Each household started torturing its own members, relatives, and slaves who were following the Prophet. The people were beaten, flogged and then thrown into the prison. The hill of Ramada and the place called Bata, had now become scenes of cruel torture. Only the Prophet was left out because he had the protection of Abu Talib^{radi Allaho anho} and Abu Bakr^{radi Allaho anho}.

Then the priest tried to tempt the Prophet into joining their religion. For this, they sent Utba Ibn Rabi'a to meet the Prophet.

"O son of my brother," said the Messenger. "You are distinguished by your qualities. Yet you have denounced our gods. I am here to make a proposition to you."

"I am listening to you, o son of Waleed." said the Prophet.

"If you are willing to acquire riches, honors, dignity, then we will offer you a fortune larger than what we have among ourselves. We shall make you

our chief, and we will consult everything with you. If you desire dominion, then we shall make you our king." said Utba.

When he had finished, the Prophet said, "Now listen to me."

"I'm listening." replied Utba.

The Prophet recited the first 13 verses of Surah Fussilat.

He praised Allah^{subhanahu wa ta'ala} and explained about the glad tidings of paradise to anyone who believed in the one true God. The Prophet then reminded him about what had happened to the people of 'Aad' and 'Thamud'. When the Prophet had finished his recitation, he said to Utba,

"This is my reply to your proposition. Now take what course you find best."

When they plan to tempt the Prophet failed, they approached his uncle Abu Talib. The Prophet's uncle tried persuading the Prophet to stop preaching to the people. But the prophet said,

"O uncle, if they were to put the sun in my right hand and the moon in my left hand to stop me from preaching Islam, I would never stop."

The Prophet, overcome by the thought that his uncle was willing to desert him, turned to depart from his home. But Abu Talib called out to the Prophet loudly. He asked him to come back. When the Prophet came back, Abu Talib told him, "Say whatever you please. By the Lord! I shall not desert you forever."

The priests from different tribes started publicly prosecuting the supporters of the Prophet. It was during this time that a Christian king named 'Al-Najashi' was ruling Abyssinia. The Prophet had heard about the

righteousness, tolerance, and hospitality of this kind ruler. When the persecution became unbearable for the people, the Prophet advised them to migrate to Abyssinia. Some 15 families emigrated to this country in small groups to avoid detection.

This is called the First Hijra in the history of Islam. This happened during the fifth year of the Prophet's mission. The emigrants received a kind reception from the king and his people. Many others who suffered at the hands of the evil priests in Makkah soon followed them. The number of people who emigrated, soon reached around one hundred.

When the priests heard about this, they were furious. They decided not to leave the emigrants in peace. They immediately sent two envoys to the King, for bringing back all of them. When the envoys met the King, he summoned the poor fugitives and asked them what they had to say.

Ja'far, the son of Abu Talib and brother of Ali, then spoke for the exiles,

"O King, we were plunged in the depth of barbarism. We adored idols, we disregarded everything, and we had no law. Then Allah raised a man among us, who is pure and honest. He taught us to worship Allah^subhanahu wa ta'ala and forbade us from worshipping the idols. He taught us to speak the truth and to be faithful. We believe in him and we have accepted his teachings. His followers were persecuted, forcing us back into worship the idols again. When we found no safety among them, we came to your kingdom, trusting you to save us from them."

When the king heard his speech, he asked the envoy to return to their land and not to interfere with the emigrants.

While his followers sought refuge in foreign lands, the Prophet continued his preaching against strict opposition. Some of them mocked at him and they asked for a sign. Then the Prophet would say, "Allah^subhanahu wa ta'ala has not sent me to work wonders. He has sent me to preach to you."

But the priest persistent didn't agree with him. They insisted that unless they saw a sign, they would not believe in his Lord. The disbelievers used to ask, "Why is he not showing any miracles like the previous Prophets?"

"Because miracles had proved inadequate to convince." answered the Prophet. "Noah^alaihi salam was sent with signs, then what happened? Where was the lost tribe of Thamud? They refused to believe in Prophet Saleh^alaihi salam, unless they showed a sign. Then the prophet caused the rocks to break and brought forth a living camel. He did what they asked for, then what happened? In anger, the people cut the camel's feet and again dared the prophet to fulfill his threat of judgment. Eventually, they all lay dead in their beds the next morning."

There are around seventeen places in the Qur'an in which the Prophet has challenged to show a sign, but he gave all of them the same answer. After some time, the priests approached Abu Talib again and asked him to abandon his nephew. But the honorable man declared his intention to protect the Prophet against any harm. The disbelievers continue to torture the Prophet and his followers wherever he went. But the Prophet kept preaching to the people, and he gained more and more followers.

THE CONVERSION OF UMER^{RADI ALLAHO ANHO}

The most notable event that happened during that time was the conversion of Umer^{radi Allaho anho}. He was one of the most rabid enemies of Islam and the Prophet. He was a tormentor of the Muslims and everyone feared him.

It is said that one day, in sheer anger, Umer resolved to kill the Prophet and he left his home with this intention. As he approached the house of the Prophet, a man stopped him. When the man learned what Umer was up to, he told him, "Your sister and her husband have embraced Islam too. Why don't you go back to your house and set it straight!"

Umer was furious to hear that his sister and her husband had become Muslims. He at once changed his direction and set out to his sister's house. As he approached their house, he could hear the sound of the Qur'an being recited.

Umer walked towards the house and knocked at the door. When the sister and her husband heard the knock at the door, they hurried to hide the book. Umer entered the house and demanded to know what was the humming sound he heard. Umer's sister replied that it was the sound of them talking to each other. But Umer knew well the sound of the Qur'an, so he asked them angrily.

"Have you become Muslims?"

"Yes, we have." answered the sister's husband.

Umer was so angry that he struck him and when his sister tried to defend her husband, he hit her face too. Blood started dribbling from her face by now. Umer's sister stood up and faced her angry brother saying, "You are an enemy of God! You have hit me just because I believe in God. Whether or not you like it, I testify that there is no god but Allah and that Muhammad, is his slave and messenger. Do whatever you will!"

Umer saw the blood running down his sister's face. Her words echoed in his ears. He demanded that the words of the Qur'an be recited to him which he had heard as he approached the house. His sister asked him to wash clean himself up before she recited those words. Umer agreed and cleaned himself and came back. When his sister recited the words from Qur'an, it filled his eyes with hot tears.

"Is this what we were up against?" he cried. "The one who has spoken these words needs to be worship." Umer left his sister's house and rushed to Allah's Messenger^{sallallaho alaihi wasallam}.

Those with the Prophet were afraid of Umer, so they tried to stop him.

The Prophet asked him, "Why did you come here, son of Khattab?"

Umer face the Prophet with humility and joy, and said, "O Messenger of God! I have come for no reason except to say I believe in God and His Messenger." The Prophet was overcome with joy and cried out that Allah is great.

Umer^{radi Allaho anho} conversion had a miraculous effect on the people of Makkah. More and more people now follow the Prophet. The disbelievers then made the life of the Prophet even more difficult. They imposed a total ban on contact with the Prophet's family. The Prophet was forced to leave

Makkah on account of the ban. During this period the Prophet and his disciples mostly stayed indoors and Islam made no progress outside. During the sacred months, when people were not violent, The Prophet came out to preach. The ban on the Prophet's family was lifted after three years and he returned to Makkah.

In the following year, his uncle, Abu Talib^{radi Allaho anho} and his wife, Khadija^{radi Allaho anha} died. The prophet had lost his guardian who protected him from enemies and Khadija^{radi Allaho anha} was his most encouraging companion. After the death of his wife, Prophet married a widowed woman, Sawda^{radi Allaho anha}. She and her husband had emigrated to Abyssinia in the early years of persecution. After her husband died, she came back to Makkah and sought Prophet's shelter. Allah's Messenger^{sallallaho alaihi wasallam} recognizing her sacrifices for Islam, extended his shelter by marrying her.

THE NIGHT OF THE JOURNEY–AL-ASRA

One calm night in Makkah, one year before the migration to Madina, Prophet Muhammad^{sallallaho alaihi wasallam} was sleeping when the Angel Jabrael^{alaihi salam} appeared before him. He opened the Prophet's chest, removed his heart and washed it with 'Zam Zam' water. He then brought a vessel made of gold, containing wisdom and faith. He emptied the vessel into the noble chest of the Prophet and then closed it up. Then, the Prophet saw a white animal, smaller than a horse but larger than a donkey, with wings on each side of its hind legs.

The Prophet mounted the animal and took off to Bait-ul-Maqdas in Jerusalem. This part of the journey is called 'Al-Isra'. After discounting the animal, the Prophet entered the Al-Aqsa mosque and prayed. He then saw his predecessors, Musa^{alaihi salam}, Isa^{alaihi salam} and Ibrahim^{alaihi salam} standing before him. The Prophet then went on to lead them in prayers. The Prophet then mounted the animal again and ascended towards the heavens. This journey is known as 'Al-Mairaj'. During the journey from the first sky to the seventh sky, Angel Jabrael^{alaihi salam} led Allah's Messenger^{sallallaho alaihi wasallam} to see a lot of scenes including the paradise and the hell. In the paradise, he saw dwelling made of pearls and their soils made of musk. He was also taken to Hell, where Allah revealed to him scenes from the future. He saw people receiving terrible punishments for different sins. Then, the angel led the Prophet to the lote tree. From this point of the journey, Prophet Muhammad^{sallallaho alaihi} ascended further without Jabrael^{alaihi salam}. Above the seventh sky, 'La-Makan' started where no being ever went. There,

Allah^{subhanahu wa ta'ala} spoke to Prophet Muhammad^{sallallaho alaihi} directly and revealed to him the last verses of 'Al-Baqara'. It is during this miraculous journey, Allah^{subhanahu wa ta'ala} gave the gift of 'Salah' to the prophet and made the daily prayers compulsory. Initially, fifty daily prayers were made compulsory. But when the Prophet received these instructions from Allah and came down, he met Musa^{alaihi salam}. Prophet Musa^{alaihi salam} asked about the gifts Allah gave to him for his 'Ummah'. When the Prophet Muhammad^{sallallaho alaihi} informed him about the 50 prayers, the Musa^{alaihi salam} said,

"Your people would not be able to perform fifty prayers each day. I tried the people before you. I had to deal with the children of Israel and it was very difficult for me. Go back to your Lord and ask him to reduce the burden on your Ummah."

The Prophet did as he was advised and went back to Allah. Allah reduced it to forty-five but when he came by the Musa^{alaihi salam} again, he suggested that to return to the Lord and ask for further reduction for the same reason. It happened multiple times, and the Prophet continued to go back and forth until Allah said, "There will be five prayers every day, and each being rewarded as ten, thus making it equivalent to 50 daily prayers."

The Prophet then met Musa^{alaihi salam} once again and informed him of the five daily prayers. Musa^{alaihi salam} repeated that he should go back again. However, the Prophet said, "I have asked my Lord till I am too shy to face him. I accept this and submit to him."

The Prophet then returned home and found his bed still warm. Allah's Messenger^{sallallaho alaihi wasallam} told about this journey to the believers and gave glad tidings to them.

THE HIJRAH TOWARDS MADINA

Islam was spreading rapidly in the region. And because of this, the disbelievers were furious. One day, leaders decided to kill the Prophet. They made a plan, in which one man was chosen from each of their tribes, and plan to attack the Prophet simultaneously at night. Allah informed the Prophet about their plans on that night and asked him to leave Makkah immediately.

Allah's Messenger^{sallallaho alaihi wasallam} left Makkah with Abu Bakr^{radi Allaho anho} in the darkness of night. They went south of Makkah to a mountain in the 'cave of Thawr'. After staying there for three nights, they traveled to Madina. This is the beginning of a new era in the life of Allah's Messenger^{sallallaho alaihi wasallam}. This is known as 'the Hijrah' meaning the migration of the Prophet from the Makkah, his home town. The Islamic calendar begins with this event.

When the disbelievers heard about this, they put up a reward of hundred camels to whoever caught the Prophet. But despite their best search parties, the Prophet arrived safely in Madina. The people of Madina gave a warm welcome to the Prophet.

One by one, the believers in Makkah left for Madina, leaving behind their properties and homes.

When the Prophet and his people settled in Madina, it was ruled by many different tribes. These tribes were constantly quarreling with each other. It

was only when the Prophet arrived, they had peace with each other. The tribesmen forgot that old feuds and were united in the bond of Islam. The Prophet in order to unite everyone in closer bonds, established between themselves a brotherhood. The first step the Prophet took after settling in Madina, was to build a mosque for the worship of Allah. Then the Prophet made a charter to make all the different people live together in an orderly fashion, clearly defining their rights and obligations. This charter represented the framework of the first commonwealth organized by the Prophet. After his emigration to Madina, the enemies of Islam increased their assault from all sides. The battle of Badr and Uhud were fought near Madina.

The fame of Allah's Messenger^{sallallaho alaihi wasallam} had by now spread far and wide. Many delegations from all parts of Arabia came to visit the Prophet. When they learned the teachings of the Prophet, they were impressed and became followers of the Prophet. The Prophet also sent many of his companions who knew the Qur'an by heart to new lands. They were sent to preach Islam to people living there.

He also wrote letters to several kings and rulers inviting them to Islam. Najashi, the king of Abyssinia, was among the first rulers who accepted Islam. This was followed by many other kings and rulers.

THE VICTORY OF MAKKAH

About two years later, at the end of 629 CE, the disbelievers violated the terms and attacked the followers of the Prophet. The men who managed to escape, took shelter in Makkah and sought the help of the Prophet to save their lives. The Prophet received their message and confirmed all the reports of the attack. The Prophet then march towards the Makkah with three thousand men. By the time he arrived outside Makkah, his followers from neighboring lands had joined him and they were over ten thousand people now.

"Except for those who are patient and do righteous deeds; those will have forgiveness and great reward." [Hud 11:11]

Before entering the city, he sent word to the citizens of Makkah that anyone who remained in his home or Abu Sufyan's home, or in the Kaa'ba would be safe. The army entered Makkah without fighting and the Prophet went directly to the Kaa'ba. He thanked Allah$^{subhanahu\ wa\ ta'ala}$ for the triumphant entry in the holy city. He then pointed at each idol with a stick he had in his hand, and said,

"The truth has come and falsehood has vanished. Surely, falsehood is bound to vanish!"

And one by one, the idols fell down. The Kaa'ba was then cleansed by the removal of all three hundred sixty idols and restored to its pristine status.

The Prophet then stood by the Kaa'ba and said, "O disbelievers, what do you think I'm about to do with you?"

"You are a nobleman, son of a noble brother."

Allah's Messenger^{sallallaho alaihi wasallam} forgave all of them saying, "I will treat you as Prophet Yusuf^{alaihi salam} treated his brothers. There is no reproach against you. Go to your homes and you are all free."

The people of Makkah accepted Islam including the staunch enemies of the Prophet. Few of his enemies had fled the city when the Prophet had made his entry. But, when they received the Prophet's assurance of no retaliation and no compulsion in religion, they came back gradually to Makkah. Within a year, 630 C.E., almost all Arabia had accepted Islam.

The Prophet performed his last pilgrimage in 632 C.E. About one hundred and thirty thousand men and women performed pilgrimage that year with him.

Two months later, The Prophet fell ill and after several days, passed away on Monday, 12th Rabbi-ul-Awwal, the eleventh year after Hijrah in Madina.

Prophet Muhammad^{sallallaho alaihi wasallam} lived a most simple, austere and modest life. He and his family used to go without a cooked meal for days, relying only on dates, dried bread, and water. During the day, he was the busiest man, as he performed his duties in many roles at once as Head of State, Chief Justice, Commander-in-Chief, Arbitrator and many many

others. He was the most devoted man at night as well. He used to spend one to two-thirds of every night in meditation and praying to Allah^subhanahu wa ta'ala for his Ummah. The Prophet's possession comprised mats, blankets, jugs and other simple things, even when he was the ruler of all Arabia.

Prophet Muhammad^sallallaho alaihi wasallam was laid to rest in Madina. A green-colored dome is built above the tomb of the Prophet and along him are early Muslim Caliphs, Abu Bakr^radi Allaho anho and Umer^radi Allaho anho. The dome is located in the south-east corner of Al-Masjid al-Nabawi (Mosque of the Prophet).

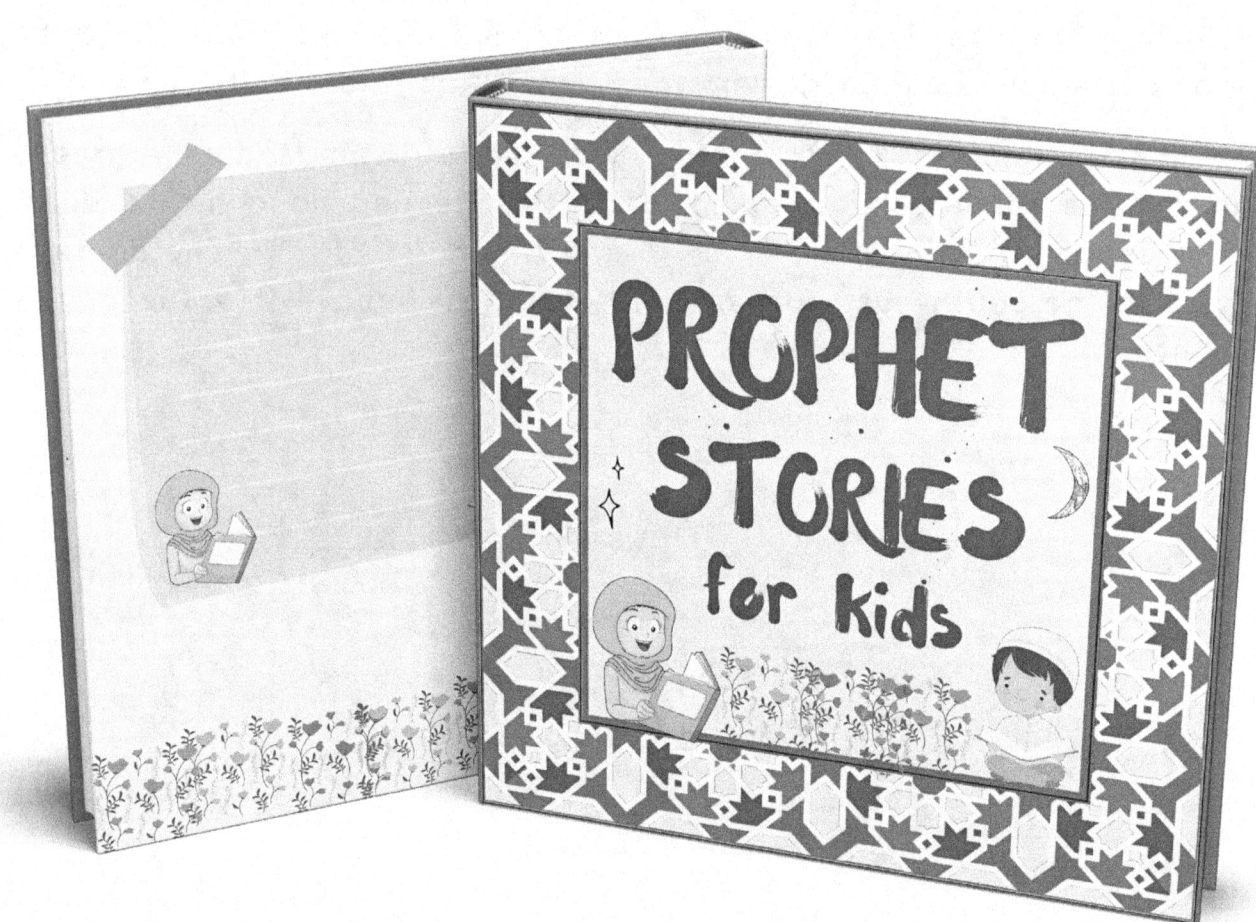

ISBN 978-1-990544-43-9

*Search ISBN on the retailer website

Premium Color Pages Hardcover

ISBN 978-1-990544-42-2

ISBN 978-1-990544-41-5

ISBN 978-1-990544-45-3

ISBN 978-1-990544-44-6

*Search ISBN on the retailer website

Premium Color Pages Hardcover

ISBN 978-1-990544-42-2 Why We Love Our Prophet Muhammad ﷺ ?

This beautifully designed book spreads the scent of the Love and Compassion shown by Holy Prophet ﷺ by his teachings and actions. His mercy encompasses all; i.e. the children, the servants, the poor, animals and birds, and especially for his Ummah (Muslim Nation).
Children will also get to know how to love back the Messenger of Allah ﷺ for his immense sacrifice and struggle for the spread of Islam, and how to extend empathy around us.

ISBN 978-1-990544-41-5 Angels & Jinn; Who are they?

Muslim children often wonder about the concept and reality of Angels and Jinn.
Are they real or is it just a myth? When and Why they were created? Are they more powerful and big than Humans? How could they help or harm us?
This beautifully designed book answers all the kid's curiosity about the reality of Angels and Jinn.
Children will learn the Islamic beliefs about them and explore the unseen universe of Allah (S.W.T) around us.

ISBN 978-1-990544-45-3 What is Religion?

Muslim children often wonder about the religions in today's modern world.
What are the differences among their followers? How they were formed and spread? Why Allah Al-Mighty sent numerous Prophets & Messengers? What is the uniqueness and authenticity of Islam and Prophet Muhammad ﷺ ?
This beautifully designed book answers all the kid's curiosity about various religions and helps parents to explain the concept of the authenticity of the last true religion; Islam.

ISBN 978-1-990544-44-6 The Great Four Rashidun Caliphs of Islam

The Life Story of Four Great Companions of Prophet Muhammad ﷺ
This beautifully designed book explains to the children about the great teachings of the Prophet Muhammad ﷺ to his Companions (R.A) that completely transformed their mindset, and later how they implemented these teachings to inspire the friends and the enemies altogether.
Learn How these Four Rightly Guided Caliphs became a beacon of leadership and created first time the concept of a welfare state for the contemporary world.

*Search ISBN on the retailer website

www.ingramcontent.com/pod-product-compliance
Lightning Source LLC
Chambersburg PA
CBHW080957120626
46546CB00010B/2938